Quick & Easy
French

Diethard Lübke

D0650720

TEACH YOURSELF BOOKS
Hodder and Stoughton

Contents

Contents

Introduction

This course of self study aims to help you understand and speak simple French, the sort of French you will need on a visit to a French-speaking country. It cannot promise that you will be speaking perfect French after a few weeks, but by giving you the most important words and expressions you will need to use on your trip, it will enable you to get a great deal more out of your time abroad.

The course consists of 20 units, each catering for a different aspect of your visit. You will not need to spend a great deal of time studying – it should be sufficient to set aside a short period each week, even if you can only manage an hour or two here and there. Go through each unit slowly, studying carefully the vocabulary and phrases it contains. Read the words aloud, look at the English translations, and refer back to the Pronunciation section. Then check your knowledge by doing the written exercises, the answers to which can be found after the units. Very soon you will find that you have acquired a basic knowledge of the language.

The exercises are of two types. Some are merely a test of memory, to see whether you have remembered how to ask a question or repeat a phrase from that particular unit. In others, you are asked to adapt the phrase or sentence in order to say what *you* want to say. For example in Unit 11 you are required to ask the waiter for several items you wish to order, and in Unit 20 you are asked to buy various items from the Chemist's. If you can do this correctly, then you have passed the 'acid test' of learning a language, which is being able to adapt what you have learnt to the situation you choose.

At the end of each unit is a short information section in English which you will find useful on your visit.

The course expects very little knowledge of grammar, but readers who are interested in how the language works will find the Introduction to French Grammar useful. This gives a very brief description of those aspects of grammar that occur in the 20 units. It is a good idea to read this briefly at the beginning, and to refer back to it as the need arises. It is also important to study the Pronunciation section before starting the course.

How to Speak French

It is worth spending some time studying correct French pronunciation and, if possible, tuning in to a French radio station to check that you have got the sounds right. Although many French words have a similar spelling to English words, the pronunciation is usually quite different. Practise saying each word out loud several times, until you are sure you have mastered the way in which it is pronounced.

1 Consonants at the end of a word are not usually pronounced. **H** is silent. Except for words of one syllable, **e** is not pronounced at the end of a word.
2 The last syllable of a word generally carries the stress.
3 French has the following accents, which can affect pronunciation: **é** (acute), **è** (grave), **ê** (circumflex), **ç** (cedilla).
4 In French, words are linked together and pronounced as one when the first word ends in a consonant and the second begins with a vowel or **h**:

   vous_allez   un_animal

   In both these examples, the final letter of the first word is pronounced, and the two words run together.

French pronunciation

Vowel sounds		*Practise saying these words*	
a	like *a* in c*a*t	bateau	assiette
â	like *à* in p*a*rk	pâté	gâteau
e, è, ê	like *e* in p*e*t	bifteck	kilomètre, crêpe
é, et,	like *ay* in d*ay*	thé	poulet
er, ez		gibier	tirez
i	like *ee* in s*ee*	voici	merci
o	like *o* in sh*o*p	homme	votre
au, o,	like *o* in g*o*	chaud	vos
eau, ô		beau	côte
eu	like *ur* in h*ur*t	bleu	heure
u	like *ew* in f*ew*	salut	rue

Nasalised vowels

These are very common in French. The vowel is pronounced through the nose, and the final **n** or **m** disappears. There is no proper English equivalent, and the sounds given below can only be a guide.

an, am, **en, em**	like sw*a*n without the *n*, pronounced through the nose	gran*d* cent	cha**mb**re ve**nd**re
in, ain, **ein, im**	like s*a*ng without the *ng*	vingt plein	terr**ain** si**mp**le
un, um **on, om**	like l*u*ng without the *ng* like s*o*ng without the *ng*	**un** pard**on**	**h**u**mb**le nom

Semi-vowels

ll	like *y* as in *y*et	bri**ller**	cui**ller**
ui	like *wee* as in s*wee*t	huit	aujourd' hui
oi	like *wo* as in *wo*n	moi	poids

Consonants

Many French consonants are similar in sound to their English equivalents. Note however the following:

c	before *i* or *e*, pronounced *s* as in *s*it	voi**ci**	**c**ette
ç	like *s* in *s*at	gar**ç**on	**ç**a
ch	like *sh* in *sh*oe	**ch**âteau	**ch**er
gn	like *ni* in o*ni*on	consi**gn**e	a**gn**eau
g	before *i* or *e* like *su* in plea*su*re	**g**arage	Bel**g**ique
j	like *su* in plea*su*re	**j**e	**j**ournal
qu	like *c* in *c*at	**qu**ai	**qu**arante
r	pronounced at the back of the tongue; in some regions, *r* is rolled.	**r**ouge	**r**apide

Introduction to French Grammar

1 The

All nouns in French are either masculine or feminine. It is not always possible to tell from the ending of a word whether it is masculine or feminine, so you should always learn each new word together with its gender.

The word for *the* with a masculine noun is **le: le sac**; with a feminine noun is **la: la valise**; with a masculine or a feminine noun beginning with a vowel is **l': l'avion**; with a masculine or a feminine noun in the plural is **les: les bagages.**

In the plural, most French nouns add an **-s,** which is not normally pronounced: **les légumes**; but some add an **-x: les châteaux.**

2 A, an, some

The word for *a, an* in French is **un** for a masculine noun: **un journal anglais; une** for a feminine noun: **une carte routière**. The word for *some/any* is **des: des tomates farcies** (*some stuffed tomatoes*); **Vous avez des prospectus?** (*Have you any brochures*?)

3 Adjectives

In French, the ending of adjectives depends on whether the nouns they accompany are masculine or feminine, singular or plural. Most adjectives take an **-e** in the feminine, but there are exceptions which should be learnt as you come across them. Most adjectives take an **-s** in the plural.

m. sing.: le **grand** château   m. plur.: les **grands** châteaux
f. sing.: la **grande** maison   f. plur.: les **grandes** maisons

In French, most adjectives come *after* the noun:

une table **libre** (*a free table*); le vin **blanc** (*white wine*)

However, some short, everyday adjectives are placed before the noun: jeune (*young*), vieux (*old*), grand (*large*), petit (*small*), bon (*good*), mauvais (*bad*).

4 To

À, meaning *to*, changes in form depending whether the noun that follows is masculine or feminine, singular or plural:

> masc.: Nous allons **au** théâtre. *We are going to the theatre.*
> fem.: À **la** gare du Nord, s.v.p. *To the Gare du Nord, please.*
> before a vowel: **à** l'église *to church*
> plural: Je vais **aux** magasins. *I am going to the shops.*

5 Of

De, meaning *of*, also changes its form:

> masc.: le Musée **du** Louvre *lit. the Museum of the Louvre*
> fem.: un voyage organisé **de la** ville *a guided tour of the town*
> before a vowel.: la porte **de** l'église *lit. the door of the church*
> plur. le circuit **des** châteaux de la Loire *a tour of the Loire castles*

Note the use of **de** in the following expressions of quantity:

> un peu **de** lait *a little milk*
> un verre **de** vin *a glass of wine*
> combien **de** tomates? *how many tomatoes?*
> une tasse **de** café *a cup of coffee*

6 This, that

The word for *this* or *that* in French is **ce** for a masculine noun, **cet** for a masculine noun beginning with a vowel, **cette** for a feminine noun and **ces** for nouns in the plural:

> **ce** chèque de voyage *this traveller's cheque*
> **cette** valise *this suitcase*
> **cet** après-midi *this afternoon*
> **ces** voitures *these cars*

7 My, your

Although the use of possessive adjectives in this book is limited to *my* and *your*, the full list is as follows:

masc.	mon	⎫	ton	⎫		son	⎫
fem.	ma	⎬ *my*	ta	⎬ *your (fam.)*		sa	⎬ *his, her*
plur.	mes	⎭	tes	⎭ (see note 8)		ses	⎭ *its*

masc.	notre ⎫		votre ⎫		leur ⎫	
fem.	notre ⎬ *our*	votre ⎬ *your*	leur ⎬ *their*
plur.	nos ⎭		vos ⎭	*(polite)*	leurs ⎭	

Note that the adjectives agree with the noun they accompany, and *not* with the person to whom the things belong.

> sa mère *his or her mother*; ses parents *his or her parents*
> son père *his or her father*; ses tantes *his or her aunts*

Here are some examples from the text:

> **Votre** passeport, s.v.p. *Your passport, please.*
> Ce sont **vos** bagages? *Is that your luggage?*
> On m'a volé **mon** argent. *Someone has stolen my money.*
> **Ma** clé, s.v.p. *My key, please.*

8   I, you, etc.

The full list of personal pronouns is as follows:

je	*I*	nous	*we*
tu	*you (fam.)*	vous	*you*
il	*he, it*	ils	*they (masc.)*
elle	*she, it*	elles	*they (fem.)*
on	*one*		

Tu is the familiar way of saying *you*, and should only be used for a child, an animal or a close friend or relation. The form used in this book is **vous**, which you will need when talking to strangers, acquaintances, and to more than one person.

Note that **on** is very common in French. It is often used in the sense of *someone*, or to mean *we*:

> On m'a volé mon argent. *Someone has stolen my money.*
> On va se promener? *Shall we go for a walk?*

9   Verbs

(*a*) Most French verbs fall into one of three categories, ending in either **-er**, **-ir**, or **-re**. Here are examples of verbs in these categories:

donner *to give*

je donne	*I give*	nous donn**ons**	*we give*
tu donne**s**	*you give*	vous donn**ez**	*you give*
il, elle donne	*he, she gives*	ils, elles donn**ent**	*they give*

finir *to finish*

je **fin**is	*I finish*	nous **fin**issons	*we finish*
tu **fin**is	*you finish*	vous **fin**issez	*you finish*
il, elle **fin**it	*he, she finishes*	ils, elles **fin**issent	*they finish*

vendre *to sell*

je **vend**s	*I sell*	nous **vend**ons	*we sell*
tu **vend**s	*you sell*	vous **vend**ez	*you sell*
il, elle **vend**	*he, she sells*	ils, elles **vend**ent	*they sell*

(*b*) There are however many irregular verbs in French, which have to be learnt as you go along. Here are some of the more common ones which are used in this book:

être
(*to be*):
je suis, tu es, il est,
nous sommes, vous êtes, ils sont
Où est la rue Dulac? *Where is Dulac Street?*

avoir
(*to have*):
j'ai, tu as, il a, nous avons, vous avez, ils ont
Vous avez un journal anglais? *Do you have an English paper?*

faire
(*to do, make*):
je fais, tu fais, il fait,
nous faisons, vous faites, ils font
Nous allons faire une excursion. *We're going on an outing (to make an excursion).*

Note the use of **faire** with expressions concerning the weather:
Quel temps **fait-il**? *What's the weather like?*
Il fait beau. *It's fine.*

perdre
(*to lose*):
je perds, tu perds, il perd,
nous perdons, vous perdez, ils perdent
J'ai perdu ma clé. *I have lost my key.*

prendre
(*to take*):
je prends, tu prends, il prend,
nous prenons, vous prenez, ils prennent
Que prenez-vous comme dessert? *What would you like for dessert?*

pouvoir
(*to be able*):
je peux, tu peux, il peut,
nous pouvons, vous pouvez, ils peuvent
Vous pouvez passer. *You can go on.*

vouloir
(*to wish, want*):
je veux, tu veux, il veut,
nous voulons, vous voulez, ils veulent

Vouloir is a very useful verb. Note these examples which can be found in the text:

Je veux changer £50. *I want to change £50.*
Comment **voulez-vous** votre steak? *How would you like your steak?*
Je voudrais louer . . . *I would like to hire . . .*

(*c*) Many of the verbs in this book are in the imperative mood, which is a verb form used frequently when talking to people. The imperative is used for giving orders or making requests, and occurs here in the **vous** form:

Allez *Go*	Suivez le guide. *Follow the guide.*
Attendez *Wait*	Appelez la police! *Call the police!*
Ouvrez *Open*	Tournez à droite. *Turn right.*
Poussez *Push*	

(*d*) Saying no
The negative is formed by putting **ne . . . pas** on either side of the verb:

Le flash **ne** marche **pas**. *The flash is not working.*
Je **ne** comprends **pas**. *I don't understand.*
Ne quittez **pas**. *Hold the line* (lit. *Do not leave*).

(*e*) Asking questions
There are several different ways of asking questions in French. Often the speaker merely raises his voice at the end of a sentence:

Vous fumez une cigarette? *Would you like a cigarette?*
(lit. *You smoke a cigarette?*)

The verb can be inverted:

Avez-vous quelque chose à déclarer? *Have you anything to declare?*

Est-ce que can be used:

Est-ce que vous avez des cartes postales? *Do you have any postcards?*

1   General Expressions

a. Yes, No   **b.** Hello, Goodbye   **c.** Please, Thank you   **d.** Mr, Mrs   **e.** The, This   **f.** I, My . . .

a.	**oui**	*yes*
	non	*no*

	Oui, monsieur.	*Yes. (to a man)*
	Non, madame.	*No. (to a lady)*

b.	**bonjour**	*good day/hello*
	au revoir	*goodbye*
	salut	*hello!*

	Bonjour, monsieur.	*Good morning/Good afternoon. (to a man)*
	Bonjour, messieurs–dames.	*Good morning/Good afternoon everyone.*
	Comment allez-vous?	*How are you?*
	Très bien, et vous?	*Very well, and you?*
	Ça va?	*How's it going?*
	Oui, ça va.	*Fine, thanks.*
	Au revoir, madame.	*Goodbye (to a lady).*

c.	**merci**	*thank you*
	s'il vous plaît (s.v.p.)	*please*
	pardon	*excuse me, pardon*

Votre passeport, s.v.p.	*Your passport, please.*
Merci, mademoiselle.	*Thank you. (to a young lady)*
Merci beaucoup.	*Thank you very much.*
Pardon, madame.	*Excuse me. (to a lady)*
Vous permettez?	*May I?*

d.	l' **homme**, la **femme**	*man, woman*
	le **monsieur (M.)**	*gentleman (Mr)*
	madame (Mme)	*Madam (Mrs, Ms)*
	la **dame**	*lady*
	mademoiselle (Mlle)	*Miss*
	le **garçon**, la **fille**	*boy, girl*

Je suis Monsieur/ Madame . . .	*I'm Mr/Mrs . . . (name)*

e.	**le** (m), **la**(f), **(l')**[1]	*the* (singular)
	les	*the* (plural)
	un (m), **une** (f)	*a, an*
	ce (cet[2]**)** (m), **cette** (f)	*this*
	c'est	*it is*
	voici/voilà	*here's, here are/there's, there are*

La valise.	*Suitcase.*
Cette valise.	*This suitcase.*

f.	**je**	*I*
	vous	*you*
	mon (m), **ma** (f)	*my*
	votre	*your*

Votre nom, monsieur?	*What is your name? (to a man)*
Voici votre clé.	*Here's your key.*
Voici mon mari.	*This is my husband.*
Voici ma femme.	*This is my wife.*
C'est votre valise?	*Is it your suitcase?*
Oui, c'est ma valise.	*Yes, it's my suitcase.*

[1] Before nouns beginning with a vowel: l'eau minérale.
[2] Before masculine nouns beginning with a vowel: cet étage.

1 General Expressions

1 You are Mr Miller. A lady asks: **C'est vous, M. Miller?** What do you answer?

2 You are Mr Miller. A man asks: **C'est vous, M. Jackson?** What do you answer?

3 You are Mrs Miller. A man asks: **C'est vous, Mme Miller?** What do you answer?

4 You are Mrs Miller. A lady asks: **C'est vous, Mme Jackson?** What do you answer?

5 How do you greet a man during the day?

6 How do you greet a lady during the day?

7 How do you say *Goodbye* to a man?

8 The customs official would like to see your passport. What does he say?

9 How do you say *Thank you* to a man?

10 How do you say *Excuse me* to a lady?

11 Mrs Miller would like to introduce her husband. What does she say?

12 Mr Miller would like to introduce his wife. What does he say?

- Courtesy in France requires the use of **monsieur**, **madame** or **mademoiselle** wherever possible. You should always address a man as **monsieur**:

     Bonjour, monsieur.

  A woman is addressed as **madame** unless you know she is not married, in which case you should use **mademoiselle**. Girls, waitresses, telephone operators, etc., should be addressed as **mademoiselle**.

     Au revoir, madame.
     Merci, mademoiselle.

- French people generally shake hands each time they meet and also when saying goodbye. When you are introduced to someone, it is polite to say:

     Enchanté(e),   monsieur/madame/mademoiselle.
     (*Pleased to meet you.*)

- **Here are some useful words and expressions**
  C'est . . .   *It is . . .*

bon	*good*	**cher**	*expensive*
mauvais	*bad*	**bon marché**	*cheap*
grand	*big*	**tôt**	*early*
petit	*small*	**tard**	*late*
facile	*easy*	**ouvert**	*open*
difficile	*difficult*	**fermé**	*closed*
lourd	*heavy*	**près**	*near*
léger	*light*	**loin**	*far*
plus	*more*	**un peu**	*a little*
moins	*less*	**beaucoup**	*a lot*
très	*very*	**avec**	*with*
trop	*too*	**sans**	*without*

2 Arriving in France

a. Customs **b**. Documents **c**. Nationality

a.

la	**douane**	*customs*
	déclarer	*declare*
les	**bagages**	*luggage*
le	**coffre**	*boot (of a car)*
le	**sac**	*handbag*
la	**valise**	*suitcase*

Avez-vous quelque chose à déclarer?	*Do you have anything to declare?*
Non, monsieur, rien à déclarer	*No, nothing to declare.*
Ce sont vos bagages?	*Is this your luggage?*
Ouvrez la valise, s'il vous plaît.	*Open your suitcase, please.*
Ouvrez le coffre.	*Open the boot.*
Ouvrez le sac.	*Open your handbag.*
C'est bien.	*That's O.K.*
Vous pouvez passer.	*Please go on.*

b.

le	**passeport**	*passport*
la	**carte grise**	*car registration papers*
le	**permis de conduire**	*driving licence*
le	**nom**	*name*
le	**prenom**	*first name*
le	**domicile**	*place of residence*

Votre passeport, s.v.p.	*Your passport, please.*
Votre nom, madame?	*Your name?*
Je m'appelle . . .	*My name is . . .*

c.

la	**nationalité**	*nationality*
la	**France**	*France*
le	**Français**	*Frenchman*
la	**Française**	*Frenchwoman*
	français	*French*
la	**Belgique**	*Belgium*
	belge	*Belgian*
la	**Suisse**	*Switzerland*
la	**Grande Bretagne**	*Great Britain*
l'	**Angleterre**	*England*
l'	**Anglais**	*English(man)*
l'	**Anglaise**	*English(woman)*
	anglais	*English*
l'	**Australie**	*Australia*
l'	**Australien/ienne**	*Australian*
l'	**Ecosse**	*Scotland*
l'	**Ecossais/aise**	*Scot*
le	**pays de Galles**	*Wales*
le	**Gallois/la Galloise**	*Welsh*
l'	**ambassade**	*embassy*
le	**consulat**	*consulate*

Vous êtes Anglais?	*Are you English?*
Oui, je suis Anglais.	*Yes, I'm English.*
Je ne comprends pas.	*I don't understand.*
Vous parlez anglais?	*Do you speak English?*
Vous avez un journal anglais?	*Do you have an English newspaper?*

2 Arriving in France

What are these called in French?

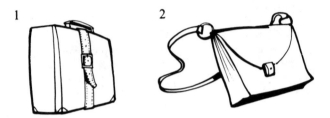

3   What does the customs official ask you?

4   You have nothing to declare. What do you answer?

5   The customs official would like you to open your boot. What does he say?

6   The customs official would like you to open your suitcase. What does he say?

7   The border guard asks you your name. What do you say?

8   The border guard would like to see your passport. What does he say to you?

9   The border guard would like to see your driving licence. What does he say?

10 You don't understand. How do you reply?

11 The border guard asks: **Vous êtes Anglais?** How do you answer?

12 The border guard is satisfied. What does he say?

What are these three countries called in French?

13 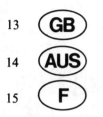 **GB**

14 **AUS**

15 **F**

16 You would like to buy an English newspaper. How do you ask the shopkeeper if he has any English newspapers?

- You are advised to check on customs allowances and purchase of duty-free goods before setting out on your trip.

- The address of the **British Embassy** in Paris is:
    4 rue Jean Rey, Paris 15ᵉ
    Australia 35 rue Faubourg St-Honoré, Paris 8ᵉ
    U.S.   2 avenue Gabriel, Paris 8ᵉ

- If you are **driving in France**, you need to carry with you the vehicle's log/registration book, a valid full driving licence and current insurance certificate (full comprehensive cover is advisable). A Green Card is not compulsory, but it will give you better cover than the minimum which applies in France. In France, locally-registered vehicles must be equipped with headlights which show a yellow beam, and visitors are advised to comply. Amber lens converters can be used or the outer surface can be painted with a yellow plastic paint (removable with a solvent). Beam deflectors are also required to adjust headlights so they do not dip to the left. It is compulsory to carry a replacement set of bulbs.

3 Driving a Car

a. Vehicles **b**. Roads C. Service Stations
d. Parking.

a.	la	**voiture**	car
	la	**caravane**	caravan
	le	**camion**	lorry
		Poids lourds	Heavy vehicles
	la	**circulation**	traffic
		aller	go, drive

Location de voitures.	Car rental.
Allons à Paris.	Let's go to Paris.

b.

la **route**	road
l' **autoroute**	motorway
le **péage**	toll
Déviation	Diversion
Travaux	Road Works
Attention	Caution
Danger	Danger
Priorité	Right of Way
Ralentir	Slow Down

La route nationale. (N)	Major road.
La route de Paris.	The road to Paris.
Bonne route!	Have a good journey!

c.

la **station-service**	service station
l' **essence**	petrol
le **gasoil**	diesel
l' **huile**	oil
les **pneus**	tyres

Super? Ordinaire?	4 star? 2 star?
Combien?	How much?
20 litres, s.v.p.	20 litres, please.
Faites le plein.	Fill it up.
Vérifiez l'huile, s.v.p.	Check the oil, please.

d.

le **parking**	parking, car park
Zone bleue	limited parking
(Disque obligatoire)	(parking disc required)
le **garage**	garage

Parking surveillé.	(Supervised) car park.
Stationnement interdit.	No parking.

Breakdowns, Accidents→20

3 Driving a Car

What are these called in French?

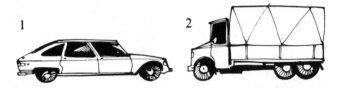

1   2

3   The petrol station attendant wants to know whether you would like 4-star or 2-star petrol. What does he ask you?

4   How do you ask the attendant to fill it up?

5   How do you ask him to check the oil and the tyres?

6   The service station attendant wishes you a good journey. What does he say?

Explain in French what the following traffic signs mean:

7

8

9

10.

11 Where does the scene in this picture take place?

- **Traffic rules** are similar to those in the UK, except that in France cars drive on the right. The old rule of **priorité à droite** (give way to the right) is gradually changing, particularly at roundabouts, but still applies in built-up areas. Note that you are not allowed to stop on open roads unless the car is driven right off the road. It is forbidden to cross a solid single line when overtaking, and on-the-spot fines can be very high. Seat-belts must be worn by the driver and front-seat passenger, and children under ten must not travel in the front of a car. A red warning triangle should be carried in case of breakdown, although this is not required if the vehicle is fitted with hazard flashers. You must also carry a complete spare bulb kit.
- **Speed limits**: Toll motorways 130 km/hr (80 mph). By-pass motorways and dual carriageways 110 km/hr (68 mph). Other roads 90 km/hr (56 mph). Towns and built-up areas 60 km/hr (37 mph).
  Rappel means continuation of the restriction.
- **Parking restrictions** vary from town to town. In some streets, cars can be parked on the side of uneven numbers for the first fortnight of the month. In **Zone Bleue** districts, parking discs – plastic cards with a clock-face which can be bought at tourist offices and kiosks – are compulsory. Always check before leaving your vehicle.

4 Finding Your Way

a. Maps **b.** In Town **c.** Streets
d. Directions

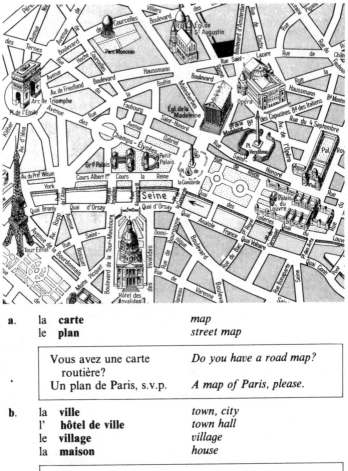

| a. | la **carte** | map |
| | le **plan** | street map |

| Vous avez une carte routière? | Do you have a road map? |
| Un plan de Paris, s.v.p. | A map of Paris, please. |

b.	la **ville**	town, city
	l' **hôtel de ville**	town hall
	le **village**	village
	la **maison**	house

La ville de Paris.	The city of Paris.
Centre ville.	City centre.
Faire un tour de ville.	Go on a sightseeing tour (of the city).

c.

la	**rue**	*street*
le	**boulevard**	*boulevard*
l'	**avenue**	*avenue*
	Sens unique	*One-way street*
la	**place**	*square*
le	**quai**	*embankment*
le	**pont**	*bridge*
le	**feu rouge**	*traffic light*
	Allez	*Go (pedestrians)*
	Attendez	*Stop (wait)*

Où est l'Avenue des Champs-Elysées?	*Where is the Champs-Elysées?*
Où habitez-vous, monsieur?	*Where do you live?*
J'habite 5 rue Dulac.	*I live at 5, Dulac Street.*

d.

la	**direction**	*direction*
	Toutes directions	*All directions*
	où est . . . ?	*where is . . . ?*
le	**virage**	*bend*
	tournez	*turn*
	à gauche	*(to the) left*
	à droite	*(to the) right*
	tout droit	*straight ahead*
le	**nord**	*north*
le	**sud**	*south*
l'	**est**	*east*
l'	**ouest**	*west*

La direction de Lille, s.v.p.?	*Which way to Lille, please?*
Pardon, monsieur, où est la rue Dulac?	*Excuse me, where is Dulac Street?*
Allez tout droit.	*Go straight ahead.*
Tournez à gauche.	*Turn left.*
Tournez à droite	*Turn right.*
C'est loin?	*Is it far?*
Non, c'est tout près.	*No, it's quite near.*

Weights and Measures→ 7, Places of Interest→15, Excursions→16

4 Finding Your Way

1 What does each letter stand for in French?

2 You want to buy a street map of Paris. What do you say?

3 You want to buy a road map. How do you ask for it?

4 You want to know how to get to the Place de la Concorde. What do you say?

5 How do you tell someone to turn right?

6 How do you tell someone to turn left?

7 How do you tell someone to go straight ahead?

8 You want to know if it's far. What do you say?

9 Which word do you see on the pedestrian signal when it is red?

10 Say the names of the largest French cities:
Paris, Marseille, Lyon, Toulouse, Bordeaux, Nice, Nantes, Strasbourg, Lille, St-Étienne, Le Havre, Nancy, Rennes, Reims.

11 You want to go to the east side of Paris. Which lane do you get into?

- Maps, town plans, lists of hotels, etc., can be obtained from the local **Syndicat d'Initiative** (see Unit 15).

- The maps published by **Michelin** and the **Institut Géographique National** (*Cartes touristiques*) are useful for finding your way in France.

- The different kinds of roads in France are:
    autoroute (A); **route nationale (N)** main road; **route européenne (E)**; **route départementale (D)** B road; **route forestière (RF)** forest road.
  Some motorways have a toll system: **autoroutes à péage.**

- Here are some common **road signs**:
    Gravillons (Loose chippings); **Chaussée déformée** (Uneven road surface); **Passage Protégé** (Right of way); **Serrez à droite** (Keep right); **Ralentir** (Slow down).
  NB Pedestrians do **not** have right of way at zebra crossings.

5 Public Transport

a. Railways **b.** Aeroplanes **c.** Ships
d. Public Transport **e.** Information

a.	les	**chemins de fer**	*railways*
	la	**gare**	*railway station*
		Consigne	*Left luggage office*
		Consigne automatique	*Left luggage lockers*
	le	**guichet**	*ticket office*
	le	**billet**	*ticket*
	la	**réservation**	*reservation*
		Grandes lignes	*main lines/long-distance trains*
		Trains de banlieue	*local trains*
	la	**voie**	*track, platform*
	le	**train**	*train*
	l'	**express**	*express train*
	le	**rapide**	*high-speed express train*
		Wagon-restaurant	*Dining car*
		Wagon-lit	*Sleeping car*
		Couchettes	*Couchettes*
	la	**salle d'attente**	*waiting room*

La gare de l'Est.	*The gare de l'Est. (= east station in Paris.)*
Un billet de seconde classe pour Paris, s.v.p.	*A second-class ticket to Paris, please.*
Un billet aller et retour.	*A return ticket.*
Voie 3.	*Platform 3.*

b.
	l' **aéroport**	*airport*
	l' **avion**	*aeroplane*
	le **vol**	*flight*

c.
	le **port**	*port*
	l' **embarcadère**	*embarkment area*
	le **bateau**	*boat/ship*
	le **pont**	*deck*
	la **cabine**	*cabin*

Le port de plaisance.	*Marina.*

d.
	le **métro**	*underground train*
	Correspondance	*Connections*
	Sortie	*Exit*
	le **R.E.R.**	*rapid transit (in Paris)*
	l' **autobus**	*bus*
	l' **arrêt d' autobus**	*bus stop*
	le **car**	*coach*
	le **taxi**	*taxi*
	Libre	*free*

Où est la station de métro?	*Where is the underground station?*
Un carnet, s.v.p.	*A book of tickets, please.*
La station de taxis.	*Taxi rank.*
À la gare du Nord, s.v.p.	*To the gare du Nord, please.*

e.
	l' **information**	*information*
	Renseignements	*Enquiries*
	l' **horaire**	*timetable*
	Départ	*Departure(s)*
	Arrivée	*Arrival(s)*
	le **retard**	*delay*

Customs→ 2, Times→ 8, Money→ 9

5 Public Transport

What sign do you look for at the railway station
1 if you need information?

2 if you want to leave your luggage?

3 if you want to take a local train?

4 if you want to take a long-distance train?

5 How do you ask for a return ticket to Paris?

6 You would like to have lunch in the train. Which carriage do you look for?

7 You want to sleep during the train journey. Which carriage do you travel in?

8 You want to go the airport. What do you say to the taxi driver?

9 You arrive at the airport and want *Departures*. What sign do you look for?

Which sign do you look for in the Paris underground

10   if you want to change trains?

11   if you want to leave the station?

12   You are at the ticket window. How do you ask for a
     book of tickets?

- The **French Railways** (SNCF) run a fast, modern
  service throughout the country. The TGV (**Trains à
  grande vitesse**) travel at very high speeds between some
  principal cities, and the TEE (**Trans-European
  Express**) provides a fast service throughout Europe for
  a supplement. It is advisable to book seats in advance
  for all long-distance journeys. Children under 4 travel
  free and under 10 travel at half price. NB Tickets
  bought in France should be validated by using the
  automatic date-stamping machine at the platform
  entrance.

- **Bus**   There are very few long-distance bus services in
  France, but local services are good. Timetables are
  available from tourist offices and at coach stations. In
  cities, fares are not standard, and several tickets may be
  required for one journey. French buses are usually
  single decker and have more standing than sitting
  space.

- **Taxis**   are only allowed to pick up from ranks. You
  should always check that they have meters. There are
  often set fares between stations.

- **Metro**   The metro is a cheap and efficient way of
  crossing Paris. There is a standard fare for any single
  journey. For several journeys, it works out cheaper to
  buy a book of tickets. RER is a very fast service
  crossing Paris, and has three lines. The fare varies
  according to length of journey in suburban districts.

6 Accommodation

a. Hotels, Camping   **b.** Hotel Rooms
c. Prices   **d.** Toilets

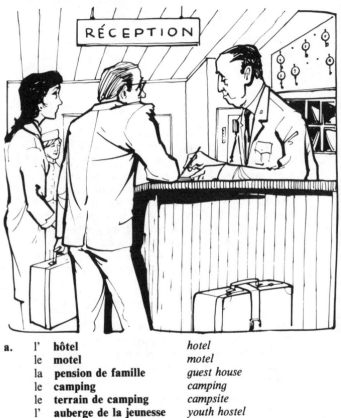

a.			
	l'	**hôtel**	*hotel*
	le	**motel**	*motel*
	la	**pension de famille**	*guest house*
	le	**camping**	*camping*
	le	**terrain de camping**	*campsite*
	l'	**auberge de la jeunesse**	*youth hostel*

Je cherche un hôtel.	*I'm looking for a hotel.*
Un bon hôtel.	*A good hotel.*
Où est le terrain de camping?	*Where is the campsite?*

b.			
	la	**réception**	*reception desk*
	la	**chambre**	*room*
	le	**lit**	*bed*

	la	**douche**	*shower*
	la	**salle de bains**	*bathroom*
	la	**clé**	*key*
	le	**rez-de-chaussée (RC)**	*ground floor*
	l'	**étage**	*floor (storey)*
	l'	**escalier**	*stairs*
	l'	**ascenseur**	*lift*

Vous avez une chambre libre?	*Do you have a room free?*
J'ai réservé une chambre pour deux personnes.	*I booked a double room.*
Une chambre pour une nuit.	*A room for one night.*
Une chambre à deux lits.	*A room with two beds.*
Avec douche et W.-C.	*With shower and toilet.*
L'hôtel est complet.	*The hotel is fully booked.*
Ma clé, s.v.p.	*My key, please.*
Le numéro de votre chambre?	*Your room number?*

c.	le	**prix**	*price*
		cher	*expensive*
	la	**note**	*bill*
	la	**pension complète**	*full board*
	la	**demi-pension**	*half board*

C'est combien, la chambre?	*How much is the room?*
Quel est le prix avec petit déjeuner?	*How much is it with breakfast?*
C'est trop cher.	*It's too expensive.*
Je veux payer maintenant.	*I'd like to pay now.*
Voici la note, monsieur.	*Here's your bill, sir.*

d.	les **toilettes,** les **W.-C.**	*toilets*
	Messieurs	*Gentlemen*
	Dames	*Ladies*
	occupé	*engaged*
	libre	*vacant*

Où sont les toilettes?	*Where are the toilets?*
Là-bas, monsieur, à gauche.	*Over there, on the left.*

Customs→ 2, Parking→ 3, Money→ 9, Meals→ 10.

6 Accommodation

What are these called in French?

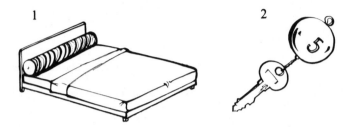

1

2

3 You're looking for a good hotel. What do you say to a passer-by?

4 How do you ask at the reception desk whether they have a vacant room?

5 You want a room with shower for one night. What do you say?

6 Ask how much the room costs with breakfast.

7 Say that you find the room too expensive.

8 What is a hotel bill called in French?

9 You are in the lift and want to go to the ground floor. Which button do you press?

10 You want to know where the toilets are. What do you say?

11 What does the sign say if the toilet is vacant?

12 What does it say if the toilet is engaged?

- There are five grades of **hotel** in France, four-star being the most luxurious. Rates are usually given for two, and breakfast is extra unless otherwise stated. Rooms with full board are usually offered for three days or more, and half board is available outside peak periods. Room prices are displayed on the backs of bedroom doors and in the *Réception*, along with breakfast and service charges. Traditionally, you pay for the room rather than the number of beds in it. All visitors are required to fill in a registration form on arrival.

- **Michelin** and the various motoring organisations produce useful hotel lists. The **Syndicats d'Initiative** also give advice about accommodation.

- **Camping/caravanning** You should only camp at official campsites. There are four grades of sites, and some of the more luxurious ones offer a wide range of facilities including swimming pools, shops, hot baths/ showers, restaurants, etc. At larger sites, tents or chalets can be hired. It is essential to book in advance for the summer months by writing to the camp, as camping is very popular in France, and most firms close for holidays either for July or August.

- **Auberges de Jeunesse** Information can be obtained from the International Youth Hostel handbook. The maximum length of stay at some hostels is three nights, at others up to a week, but this varies according to the season. It is essential to book for July and August.

- Note that electric **voltage** varies in France, but is generally 220 volts (including graded campsites). Two-pin plugs are widely used, and adapters should be purchased.

7 Numbers, Weights and Measures

a. Numbers **b.** Weights and Measures

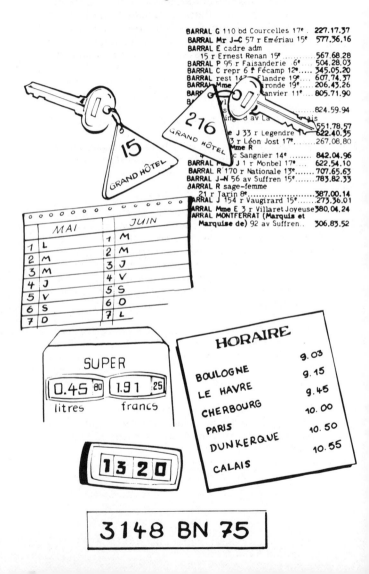

BARRAL G 110 bd Courcelles 17ᵉ . **227.17.37**
BARRAL Mr J—C 57 r Emériau 15ᵉ **577.36.16**
BARRAL E cadre adm
  15 r Ernest Renan 15ᵉ **567.68.28**
BARRAL P 95 r Faisanderie 6ᵉ . **504.28.03**
BARRAL C repr 6 r Fécamp 12ᵉ..... **345.05.20**
BARRAL rest 142 r Flandre 19ᵉ....... **607.74.37**
BARRAL Mme r Gironde 19ᵉ. **206.43.26**
BARS G r Janvier 11ᵉ ... **805.71.90**
B...
s...
........**824.59.94**
... 8 av La...ais
.... **551.78.57**
...e J 33 r Legendre 1... **622.40.55**
...3 r Léon Jost 17ᵉ........**267.08.80**
... Mme R
...c Sangnier 14ᵉ **842.04.96**
BARRAL P ... J 1 r Monbel 17ᵉ **622.54.10**
BARRAL R 170 r Nationale 13ᵉ....... **707.65.63**
BARRAL J—N 56 av Suffren 15ᵉ.......**783.82.33**
BARRAL R sage-femme
  21 r Jarin 8ᵉ........................**387.00.14**
ARRAL J 154 r Vaugirard 15ᵉ.......**273.36.01**
ARRAL Mme E 3 r Villaret Joyeuse **380.04.24**
ARRAL MONTFERRAT (Marquis et
  Marquise de) 92 av Suffren.. **306.83.52**

MAI		JUIN	
1	L	1	M
2	M	2	M
3	M	3	J
4	J	4	V
5	V	5	S
6	S	6	D
7	D	7	L

SUPER
0.45 80 | 1.91 25
litres | francs

1 3 2 0

HORAIRE
BOULOGNE   9.03
LE HAVRE   9.15
CHERBOURG   9.45
PARIS   10.00
DUNKERQUE   10.50
CALAIS   10.55

3148 BN 75

a.

0 zéro	10 dix	20 vingt
1 un	11 onze	21 vingt et un
2 deux	12 douze	22 vingt-deux
3 trois	13 treize	23 vingt-trois . . .
4 quatre	14 quatorze	30 trente
5 cinq	15 quinze	31 trente et un
6 six	16 seize	32 trente-deux
7 sept	17 dix-sept	33 trente-trois . . .
8 huit	18 dix-huit	40 quarante
9 neuf	19 dix-neuf	50 cinquante

60 soixante		200 deux cents
70 soixante-dix (= 60 + 10)		210 deux cent dix
71 soixante et onze		300 trois cents
72 soixante-douze		400 quatre cents
73 soixante-treize . . .		500 cinq cents
80 quatre-vingts (= 4 × 20)		1 000 mille
81 quatre-vingt-un		2 000 deux mille
82 quatre-vingt-deux . . .		2 010 deux mille dix
90 quatre-vingt-dix		3 000 trois mille
99 quatre-vingt-dix-neuf		10 000 dix mille
100 cent		100 000 cent mille
101 cent un		1 000 000 un million

b.

le **gramme**	*gram*
le **kilo**	*kilogram*
le **litre**	*litre*
le **mètre**	*metre*
le **kilomètre**	*kilometre*
le **centimètre**	*centimetre*
combien de . . . ?	*how many. . . ?*
peu	*a little*
beaucoup	*a lot*

Deux cents grammes de beurre.	*200 grams of butter.*
Combien de tomates?	*How many tomatoes?*
Un kilo de tomates, s.v.p.	*A kilo of tomatoes, please.*
50 kilomètres jusqu'à Paris.	*50 kilometres to Paris.*
Un peu de lait.	*A little milk.*

Times and Dates→ 8

7 Numbers, Weights and Measures

Which rooms are these hotel guests staying in?

1 M. Martin

2 M. Dubois

3 Mr Miller

4 Mr Jackson

Which platform do these trains leave from?

HORAIRE		Voie
BOULOGNE	9.03	5
LE HAVRE	9.15	8
CHERBOURG	9.45	2
PARIS	10.00	1
BOULOGNE	10.50	5
CALAIS	10.55	3

5 The train to **Boulogne**.
6 The train to **Le Havre**.
7 The train to **Cherbourg**.
8 The train to **Paris**.
9 The train to **Calais**.

10 Read out the following distances in French:
   (a)   Paris–Chartres   90 km
   (b)   Paris–Lille   220 km
   (c)   Paris–Strasbourg   460 km
   (d)   Paris–Marseille   780 km
   (e)   Paris–Bordeaux   560 km
   (f)   Paris–Brest   580 km

11 Where does M. Dubois live? Read out his address in
    French:

                33, rue de Verdun
                75 046 Paris

12 How much does this packet of butter weigh?
13 How much coffee is in this packet?
14 You want to buy a kilo of tomatoes. What do you
    say?

– In France, the **metric system** of weights and measures
  is used:

kilograms		pounds	grams		ounces
1	=	2.2	100	=	3.5
5	=	11.0	250	=	9.0
litres		**gallons**	**kilometres**		**miles**
1	=	.22	1	=	.62
5	=	1.1	20	=	12.4

NB 1 lb = 0.45 kg; 1 pint = 0.57 litres;
1 gal. = 4.54 litres; 1 mile = 1.6 km; 8 km = 5 miles.

8 Times and Dates

a. Telling the Time **b.** Times of the Day
c. Week and Month

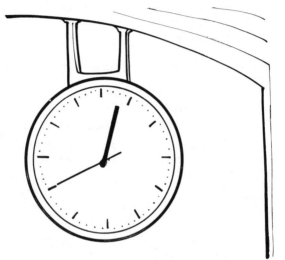

a.

la	**montre**	*watch*
l'	**horloge**	*clock*
l'	**heure (h)**	*hour*
la	**minute**	*minute*
le	**moment**	*moment*

Quelle heure est-il?	*What's the time?*
Il est 10 heures du matin.	*It's 10 o'clock in the morning.*
Il est 10 heures et demie.	*It's 10.30. (half past ten)*
Il est 10 heures et quart.	*It's quarter past ten.*
Il est 10 heures moins le quart.	*It's quarter to ten. (Lit. ten hours less a quarter)*
Il est 2 heures de l'après-midi.	*It is 2 in the afternoon.*
À 9 heures du soir.	*At 9 o'clock at night.*
À 22 heures.	*At 10 p.m.*

Une heure.	*One hour.*
Une demi-heure.	*Half an hour.*
Un quart d'heure.	*Quarter of an hour.*
Un moment, s.v.p.	*Just a moment, please.*

b.

le	**jour**	*day*
le	**matin**	*morning*
	midi	*noon*
l'	**après-midi**	*afternoon*
le	**soir**	*evening*
la	**nuit**	*night*
	minuit	*midnight*
	aujourd'hui	*today*
	demain	*tomorrow*
	hier	*yesterday*
	tous les jours	*every day*

Quand partez-vous, monsieur?	*When are you leaving?*
Demain matin.	*Tomorrow morning.*
Ce soir à 9 heures.	*At 9 o'clock this evening.*
À quelle heure part le train?	*When does the train leave?*
À midi.	*At midday.*

c.

la	**semaine**	*week*
	lundi	*Monday*
	mardi	*Tuesday*
	mercredi	*Wednesday*
	jeudi	*Thursday*
	vendredi	*Friday*
	samedi	*Saturday*
	dimanche	*Sunday*
le	**mois**	*month*
l'	**an**	*year*

La semaine prochaine.	*Next week.*
La semaine dernière.	*Last week.*
Fermé le lundi.	*Closed on Mondays.*
Mardi le 14 juillet.	*Tuesday, July 14th.*
Jeudi le 22 août.	*Thursday, August 22nd.*

Public Transport→ 5, Numbers→ 7

8 Times and Dates

1 You want to know what time it is. What do you say?

2 Say what time of the morning it is for each of the clocks below.

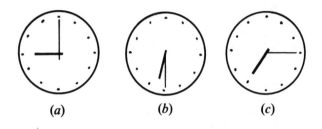

    (a)   (b)   (c)

3 Say what time of the afternoon or evening it is.

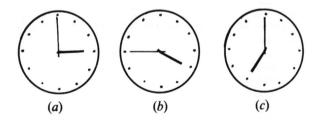

    (a)   (b)   (c)

4 How do you say in French:
(a) 20 minutes; (b) half an hour; (c) 10 days; (d) 6 months?

5 Someone asks when you are leaving. Say that you are leaving at midnight.

6 You want to know what time the plane leaves. What do you say?

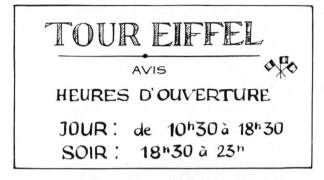

7   What are the opening times of the Eiffel Tower? Read them aloud.

8   When was this newspaper published?

  – The **months of the year** are: janvier, février, mars, avril,
    mai, juin, juillet, août, septembre, octobre, novembre,
    décembre.
    Unlike in English, days of the week and months of the
    year are not written with initial capital letters in
    French.
    Note that *lundi* = on Monday, and *le lundi* = on
    Mondays.
  – The **24-hour clock** is used for official purposes (on
    timetables etc.):
      13.00 = 1 pm; 18.30 = 6.30 pm, and so on.

9 Money and Shopping

a. Money **b.** At the Bank, Changing Money
c. Shopping **d.** Paying

a.	l'	**argent**	*money*
	la	**monnaie**	*small change*
	le	**billet**	*note*
	la	**pièce**	*coin*
	le	**franc (F)**	*franc*
	le	**centime**	*centime*

50 centimes, s.v.p.	*50 centimes, please.*
20 francs, s.v.p.	*20 francs, please.*

b.

la	**banque**	*bank*
le	**bureau de change**	*currency exchange*
	changer	*change, exchange*
le	**chèque de voyage**	*traveller's cheque*
la	**carte de crédit**	*credit card*

Je veux changer 50 livres.	*I'd like to change £50.*
1000 francs belges.	*1000 Belgian francs.*
200 francs suisses.	*200 Swiss francs.*
Je veux encaisser ce chèque de voyage.	*I'd like to cash this traveller's cheque.*

c.

	acheter	*buy*
le	**magasin**	*shop*
le	**grand magasin**	*department store*
le	**supermarché**	*supermarket*
le	**marché**	*market*
	Libre-service	*Self-service*
	Entrée libre	*No obligation to buy*

Que désirez-vous?	*May I help you?*
Je voudrais . . .	*I'd like . . .*
Je veux acheter un pullover.	*I'd like a pullover.*
Vous avez des chemises?	*Do you have any shirts?*
Et avec ça?	*Anything else?*
Merci beaucoup.	*Thank you very much.*

d.

le	**prix**	*price*
	payer	*pay*
la	**caisse**	*cash desk*
	cher	*expensive*
	bon marché	*cheap*
	gratuit	*free*

C'est combien?	*How much is it?*
C'est 20 francs.	*It's 20 francs.*
C'est (trop) cher.	*That's (too) expensive.*
Ça fait combien?	*How much does that come to?*
Vous payez à la caisse.	*You can pay the cashier.*

Numbers, Weights and Measures → 7, Clothing → 19

9 Money and Shopping

1 You want to change some money. What sign do you look for?

2 You enter a shop. What does the shop assistant ask you?

3 You want to know whether they have any pullovers. What do you say?

4 You want to know how much a shirt costs. What do you say?

5 Say that the shirt costs 150 francs.

6 The shop assistant asks if you would like anything else. What does she say?

7 The assistant tells you to pay at the cash desk. What does she say?

8 Ask how much it comes to.

9 Here is a receipt from a large Paris department store.

(a) How much did the first item cost?
(b) How much did the second item cost?
(c) How much did the customer pay altogether?

10 Read out the prices of these three dresses in French:

(a) 325 F   (b) 239 F   (c) 219 F

- **Banks** are open from 9 am to noon and two to four on weekdays, and closed either Saturdays (in large towns) or Mondays. Banks close early on the day before a public holiday, and sometimes on the day after (see list in unit 15).

- **Shops** are open from 9 am to 6.30 or 7.30 pm. Food shops open at 7 am. Many shops close all or half-day on Monday. Some food shops (especially bread shops) open on Sunday mornings. Most towns have a Saturday fruit and vegetable market. Many hyper-markets, which are often a little way out of the town, stay open until 9 or 10 pm from Monday to Saturday. Shops in small towns often close from noon to two.

- Here are the names of some common shops:

Alimentation ⎫ _grocer's_ **l'épicerie** ⎭	**la boucherie** _butcher's_
la boulangerie _baker's_	**la poissonnerie** _fishmonger's_
la pâtisserie _cake shop_	**la quincaillerie** _hardware_
la crémerie _dairy_	**la pharmacie** _chemist's_
la librairie _bookshop_	**la cordonnerie** _shoe repairs_

10 Meals

a. Meals **b.** Tableware **c.** Breakfast **d.** Snacks.

a.	le	**repas**	*meal*
	le	**petit déjeuner**	*breakfast*
	le	**déjeuner**	*lunch*
	le	**goûter**	*afternoon snack*
	le	**dîner**	*dinner, supper*
	le	**souper**	*evening snack*
		manger	*eat*
		boire	*drink*
	la	**salle à manger**	*dining-room*
b.	la	**tasse**	*cup*
	le	**bol**	*bowl*
	le	**verre**	*glass*
	la	**bouteille**	*bottle*
	la	**carafe**	*jug*
	l'	**assiette**	*plate, dish*
	la	**soupière**	*soup bowl*
	la	**cuiller**	*spoon*
	la	**fourchette**	*fork*
	le	**couteau**	*knife*

	la	**serviette**	*napkin*
	la	**nappe**	*table cloth*

Une tasse de café.	*A cup of coffee.*
Une bouteille de vin.	*A bottle of wine.*
Un verre d'eau.	*A glass of water.*

c.

le	**pain**	*bread*
la	**baguette**	*French bread*
le	**croissant**	*croissant*
le	**petit pain**	*roll*
le	**beurre**	*butter*
la	**confiture**	*jam/marmalade*
le	**café**	*coffee*
le	**thé**	*tea*
le	**chocolat**	*hot chocolate*
le	**jus de fruit**	*fruit juice*

Café ou thé?	*Coffee or tea?*
Un café au lait.	*Coffee with a large portion of hot milk.*
Thé nature? Au citron?	*Tea with or without lemon?* (= *Plain tea? Tea with lemon?*)
La confiture de fraises.	*Strawberry jam.*

d.

le	**sandwich**	*sandwich (made with a baguette)*
le	**croque-monsieur**	*toasted sandwich*
le	**jambon**	*ham*
la	**crêpe**	*crêpe, pancake*
la	**saucisse**	*sausage*
l'	**omelette**	*omelette*
les	**frites**	*chips*

Vous avez des sandwichs?	*Do you have any sandwiches?*
Un sandwich au jambon.	*A ham sandwich.*
Un sandwich au fromage.	*A cheese sandwich.*
Des saucisses de Francfort.	*Frankfurters/Hot dogs.*
Une omelette aux fines herbes.	*An omelette with herbs.*

Paying → 9, Restaurants → 11, Drinking → 14

10 Meals

1 What are the three meals of the day called in French?

2 What are the following called in French?

(a) *(b)* *(c)* *(d)* *(e)* *(f)*

3 What are these called in French?

(a) *(b)* *(c)*

4   You'd like a glass of wine. What do you say to the waiter?

5   How would you ask for a loaf of French bread?

6   You want coffee with milk. What do you ask for?

7   Say that you would like a ham omelette.

8   How would you ask for a cheese sandwich?

- **Meals**   Breakfast is a very light meal of bread and butter, and a drink of coffee or hot chocolate. Sometimes croissants are eaten. The main meal is traditionally lunch at 12 or 12.30 (**le déjeuner** or **le repas de midi**.) Many offices, shops and banks still close at lunchtime so that employees can go home, though this habit is being discouraged. **Le goûter** is a tea-time snack of bread and jam or chocolate for children. The main evening meal is **le dîner,** usually eaten between 7 and 8. **Le souper** is a light snack, perhaps following an evening at the theatre.

- **Food** is considered a very important aspect of French life, and meals are taken very seriously. Each area has its own specialities, which are served at home and in local restaurants. You do not have to go to an expensive restaurant to eat well. Among the best value are the meals served in the **relais routiers,** which are the cafés for long-distance drivers.

- Note that **prices for drinks** vary according to where you sit in a bar or café. They are cheapest standing at the bar, and most expensive sitting outside on the *terrasse*.

11 Restaurants

a. Restaurants **b.** Service, Menu
c. Seasonings **d.** The Bill

a.	le	**restaurant**	*restaurant*
	le	**café**	*café, bar (for drinks only)*
	le	**bar**	*bar (for drinks only)*
	le	**salon de thé**	*café, tea shop*
	la	**table**	*table*
	la	**chaise**	*chair*
	la	**terrasse**	*terrace*

C'est pour manger.	*We'd like to eat.*
Vous êtes combien?	*How many persons?*
Avez-vous une table pour 3 personnes?	*Do you have a table for 3?*
Voilà une table libre.	*There's a free table.*

b.

la	**carte**	*menu*
	commander	*order*
le	**menu à prix fixe**	*set meal, fixed-price meal*
l'	**apéritif**	*cocktail, before-dinner drink*
le	**hors-d'œuvre**	*appetizer, hors d'œuvre*
le	**plat**	*course, dish*
le	**dessert**	*dessert*
le	**fromage**	*cheese*
le	**café**	*coffee*
la	**carte des vins**	*wine list*

La carte, s.v.p.	*Could we have the menu, please?*
Je prends le menu 3.	*I'll take the set meal no. 3.*
Que prenez-vous comme dessert?	*What would you like for dessert?*
Et comme boisson?	*What would you like to drink?*
Voici le plateau de fromage.	*(Here's) The cheese platter.*

c.

le	**sucre**	*sugar*
le	**sel**	*salt*
le	**poivre**	*pepper*
l'	**huile**	*oil*
le	**vinaigre**	*vinegar*

d.

le	**garçon**	*waiter*
l'	**addition**	*bill*
	service (non) compris	*service (not) included*
le	**pourboire**	*tip*

Garçon, s.v.p.	*Waiter!*
Mademoiselle, s.v.p.	*Waitress!*
Apportez-moi l'addition, s.v.p.	*Bring me the bill, please.*

Toilets→ 6, Paying→ 9, Meals→ 10, Drinking→ 14

11 Restaurants

1 Where do you go
   (a) if you want lunch?
   (b) if you only want a drink?
   (c) if you want coffee and cakes?

2 What are these called in French?

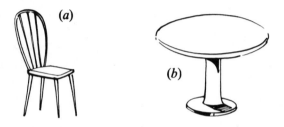
(a)
(b)

3 You are in a restaurant. Ask the waiter if he has a table for two.

4 Tell the waiter you would like to see the menu and the wine list.

5 Say you would like to order the set meal no. 1.

6 The waiter asks what you would like to drink. What does he say?

7 Attract the waiter's attention and ask him to bring you the oil and vinegar.

8 How do you ask for your bill?

9   What are the following called in French?

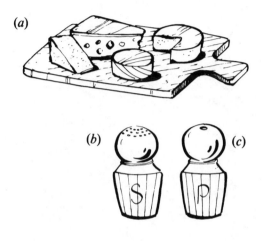

(a)

(b)   *(c)*

- All **restaurants** must display priced menus outside.
  Most offer a set menu which often represents the best
  value. Look for the **plat du jour** (dish of the day) or
  menu à prix fixe. There is usually a cover charge (*le
  couvert*) for each person, and service is not included
  unless stated (*service compris*). In the tourist season, a
  menu gastronomique may offer regional specialities.

- It is usual to leave a **tip** of ten or fifteen per cent for the
  waiter.

- **French cheese** is famous throughout the world. Some
  of the best-known cheeses are Gruyère, Boursin, Bleu
  de Bresse, Roquefort, Brie, Camembert, Coulommiers,
  and Crottin de Chavignol (goat's milk cheese). When
  offered the cheese platter, you are expected to cut a
  small slice from one (or at the most two) of the cheeses.
  This is eaten with plain bread, rather than biscuits.

12　Starters, Meat, Fish

a. Starters　**b.** Meat　**c.** Poultry, Eggs　**d.** Fish.

a.	la	**soupe**	soup
	le	**potage**	(thick) soup
	le	**bouillon**	clear (meat) soup, bouillon
	le	**consommé**	clear soup, consommé
	les	**crudités**	raw vegetable salad

La soupe à l'oignon.	*Onion soup.*
Le potage bonne femme.	*Vegetable soup.*
Le pot-au-feu.	*Beef broth.*
Les hors d'œuvres variés.	*Salami and cold meats.*

b.

la	**viande**	*meat*
	Bœuf	*Beef*
	Veau	*Veal*
	Porc	*Pork*
	Gibier	*Game*
la	**côtelette**	*chop*
l'	**escalope**	*veal cutlet*
l'	**entrecôte**	*rib steak*
le	**bifteck**	*(beef)steak*
le	**steak**	*steak*
le	**pâté**	*pâté*
	Cuisses de Grenouille	*Frog's legs*
	Escargots	*Snails*
la	**sauce**	*sauce, gravy*

Comment voulez-vous votre steak?	*How do you like your steak?*
Saignant? À point? Bien cuit?	*Rare? Medium? Well done?*
Le gigot d'agneau.	*Leg of lamb.*
Le ragout de bœuf.	*Stew.*
Le pâté de foie.	*Liver pâté.*

c.

	Volaille	*poultry*
le	**poulet**	*chicken*
le	**canard**	*duck*
l'	**œuf**	*egg*

Le poulet rôti.	*Roast chicken.*
Les œufs sur le plat.	*Fried eggs.*
Une omelette aux champignons.	*A mushroom omelette.*

d.

	Poissons	*Fish*
la	**sole**	*sole*
le	**cabillaud**	*cod*
le	**maquereau**	*mackerel*
	Fruits de mer	*Shellfish*
les	**crevettes**	*shrimps*
	Moules	*Mussels*
	Huîtres	*Oysters*
la	**bouillabaisse**	*fish stew*

Ask for the following in French:

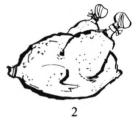

1

2

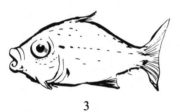

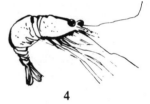

3

4

What do you say to the waiter:

5 If you want vegetable soup?

6 If you want pâté?

7 If you want the veal cutlet?

8 If you want your steak well done?

9 If you want your steak rare?

10 If you want fried eggs?

11 If you want fish stew?

12 Translate into English the names of the following
    ingredients which are being used in the above recipe:

> Fromage
> Pain blanc
> Vin blanc
> Oignons
> Poivre
> Sel
> Bouillon

— Lunch and dinner are often three- or four-course meals in
France, with starter, main course, cheese, then dessert.
Bread is eaten with most courses, and you are expected to
hold onto your knife and fork for more than one course.

13 Vegetables, Fruit, Desserts

a. Vegetables **b.** Fruit **c.** Desserts, Sweets.

a.	**Légumes**	*Vegetables*
les	**pommes de terre**	*potatoes*
les	**frites**	*chips*
les	**carottes**	*carrots*
les	**tomates**	*tomatoes*
les	**petits pois**	*green peas*
les	**haricots verts**	*runner beans*

l'	**artichaut**	*artichoke*
l'	**oignon**	*onion*
l'	**ail**	*garlic*
le	**chou**	*cabbage*
les	**champignons**	*mushrooms*
la	**salade**	*lettuce*
le	**riz**	*rice*

Des tomates farcies.	*Stuffed tomatoes.*
Les choux de Bruxelles.	*Brussels sprouts.*
L'artichaut à la vinai-grette.	*Artichokes in vinaigrette.*
La salade Niçoise.	*Salad with tuna and olives.*

b.

	Fruits	*Fruit*
la	**pomme**	*apple*
la	**poire**	*pear*
le	**citron**	*lemon*
les	**cerises**	*cherries*
les	**fraises**	*strawberries*
les	**framboises**	*raspberries*
l'	**orange**	*orange*
la	**banane**	*banana*
le	**melon**	*melon*
les	**raisins**	*grapes*

Les fraises au sucre.	*Strawberries with sugar.*
Le melon glacé.	*Iced melon.*

c.

	Glaces	*Ice cream*
la	**tarte**	*tart*
le	**gâteau**	*cake*
la	**pâtisserie**	*pastry*
la	**crème**	*cream*
le	**chocolat**	*chocolate*
le	**bonbon**	*sweet*

Que voulez-vous?	*What would you like?*
Vanille? Praline? Pistache?	*Vanilla? Nut? Pistachio?*
La tarte aux pommes.	*Apple tart.*

13 Vegetables, Fruit, Desserts

What are the following in French? Say you like them.
Start: **J'aime ...**
Example: 1 Les haricots verts. J'aime les haricots verts.

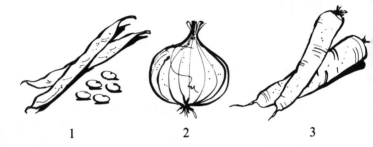

1   2   3

4   5   6

7   8   9

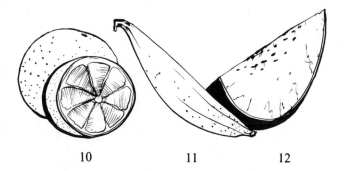

10   11   12

13 Say you would like stuffed tomatoes.

14 Ask the waiter to bring you the cream.

15 You would like an ice cream. What sign do you look for?

16 You would like vanilla and chocolate. What do you ask the ice-cream man?

- Vegetables and salads are often served separately from the meat course, and sometimes constitute a course by themselves. It is common to be offered fruit for dessert, rather than stodgy puddings. Note that in France, dessert usually follows the cheese course.

- The vocabulary in Units 12 and 13 has covered many of the items to be found on a French menu, and will help you with your choice of dishes in a restaurant.

14 Drinking and Smoking

a. Non-alcoholic Beverages
b. Alcoholic Beverages   **c.** Smoking

a.
les	**boissons**	*drinks*
l'	**eau minérale**	*mineral water*
le	**jus**	*juice*
l'	**orangeade**	*orange juice*
le	**café**	*coffee*
le	**thé**	*tea*

J'ai soif.	*I'm thirsty.*
Un jus de pommes.	*An apple juice.*
Un citron pressé.	*Fresh lemon with sugar and water.*
Un café au lait.	*Coffee with hot milk.*
Un café crème	*Coffee with cream.*
Un thé nature.	*Plain tea.*
Un thé au citron.	*Tea with lemon.*

b.
la	**bière**	*beer*
la	**vin**	*wine*
le	**champagne**	*champagne*
le	**cidre**	*cider*
la	**liqueur**	*liqueur*
le	**cognac**	*cognac*
la	**bouteille**	*bottle*
l'	**ouvre-bouteilles**	*bottle opener*
le	**tire-bouchon**	*cork screw*

Une bière blonde.	*A light beer.*
Le vin blanc/rosé/rouge.	*White wine/rosé/red wine.*
Une bouteille de vin.	*A bottle of wine.*
Une demi-bouteille de vin.	*A half-bottle of wine.*

c.
la	**cigarette**	*cigarette*
le	**cigare**	*cigar*
le	**briquet**	*lighter*
l'	**allumette**	*match*
le	**cendrier**	*ashtray*
le	**bureau de tabac**	*tobacconist*

Vous fumez une cigarette?	*Would you like a cigarette?*
Un paquet de cigarettes.	*A packet of cigarettes.*
Avec ou sans filtre?	*With or without filter?*
Une boîte d'allumettes.	*A box of matches.*
Défense de fumer.	*No smoking.*

Meals → 10

14   Drinking and Smoking

1   The waiter asks if you would like coffee or tea. What does he say?

2   Ask for coffee with cream.

3   How do you ask for a packet of cigarettes and a box of matches?

4   What do you say if you want to offer someone a cigarette?

What are these called in French?

5

6

7

8

9

10

You have ordered a meal. The waiter asks if you would like anything to drink: *Et comme boisson?* Say you would like the items below.

Start: **Je voudrais...** (*I would like...*).

11   an apple juice.

12   a bottle of red wine.

13   a light beer.

14   a glass of cognac.

- **Wine** is drunk at mealtimes (children drink wine with water), and France is famous for its quality and variety of wines. Local *vin de table* (table wine) usually accompanies a meal, and the top quality wines are kept for special occasions. The three qualities of wine are: *vin de pays* (cheap, local); *VDQS* (grapes from a particular area); *appellation contrôlée* (top quality, with a government guarantee).

- The most famous **wine-making areas** are Bordeaux, Burgundy, Champagne, Loire, Alsace and Rhône.

- **Cigarettes and tobacco** can be bought at a **bureau de tabac,** or **café-tabac.** Look for the red carrot-shaped sign.

NB Never drink water from
a tap labelled *Eau non potable.*

15 Sightseeing and Entertainment

a. Tourism **b.** Places of Interest
c. Entertainment **d.** Admission.

Mont-Saint-Michel

a.

le	**touriste**	*tourist*
le	**syndicat d'initiative (S.I.)**	*tourist information office*
le	**prospectus**	*brochure*
l'	**agence de voyages**	*travel agency*

Où est le syndicat d'initiative?	*Where is the tourist office?*
Vous avez des prospectus?	*Do you have any brochures?*

b.

les	**curiosités**	*sights*
le	**musée**	*museum*
le	**château**	*castle, palace*
le	**palais**	*palace*
l'	**église**	*church*
la	**cathédrale**	*cathedral*
la	**tour**	*tower*
le	**pèlerinage**	*pilgrimage*

Le musée du Louvre.	*The Louvre.*
Visiter la Vénus de Milo et la Joconde.	*See the Venus de Milo and the Mona Lisa*
Visiter le château de Versailles.	*Visit the palace of Versailles.*

c.

le	**théâtre**	*theatre*
le	**cinéma**	*cinema*
la	**boîte de nuit**	*night club*
la	**salle de concert**	*concert hall*
la	**fête**	*festival*
le	**stade**	*stadium*

Nous allons au théâtre.	*We are going to the theatre.*
À quelle heure commence le spectacle?	*What time does the performance start?*

d.

les	**heures d'ouverture**	*opening hours*
	ouvert	*open*
	fermé	*closed*
l'	**entrée**	*entrance*
la	**sortie**	*exit*
	Poussez	*push*
	Tirez	*pull*
la	**caisse**	*cashier, ticket window*
le	**billet**	*ticket*
le	**guide**	*guide*
	visiter	*visit, see, tour*

Votre billet, s.v.p.	*Your ticket, please.*
Un voyage organisé de la ville.	*A conducted tour of the town.*
Suivez le guide.	*Follow the guide.*
Sortie de secours.	*Emergency exit.*

15 Sightseeing and Entertainment

Do you know these tourist attractions in Paris? Can you
name them?

1

2

3

4

5   You'd like advice on reserving a hotel room and brochures on places of interest. Where can you find help?

6   You're going to the theatre. Your friend asks what time the performance starts. What does he say?

7   Tell him that it starts at seven o' clock.

You're visiting a museum. Which sign do you look for

8   to find out the opening times?

9   when you want to buy admission tickets?

10   Which sign indicates the entrance?

11   Which sign indicates the exit?

12   The museum, the shop or the garage are closed. What does the sign say?

- There are **Syndicats d'Initiative** and **Offices de Tourisme** in almost every town and resort in France, and they can advise on accommodation, restaurants, entertainment, timetables and so on.
- **Museums** are closed on public holidays (see list below). Many museums close all day on Tuesdays. Some are free on Wednesdays, or Sundays; for others there is a 50 % reduction on Sundays. There are reductions for children, OAPs and the unemployed.
- **Cinema and theatre** Note that it is customary to tip the usherette who shows you to your seat. Performances begin rather late in France. There is no smoking in theatres and cinemas. Most night-clubs are rather expensive and frequented by businessmen.
- There are many special events and festivals taking place each year in France, and a list is available from the French Government Tourist Office, 178 Piccadilly, London W1.
- **Jours fériés** (public holidays): New Year's Day, Easter Monday, May Day, Ascension Day, Whit Monday, Bastille Day (14 July), Feast of the Assumption (15 August), All Saints' Day (1 November), Armistice Day (11 November) and Christmas Day.

16 Excursions and Recreation

a. Excursions **b.** Scenery **c.** Sports
d. Photography

a.

l'	**excursion**	*excursion, outing*
le	**circuit**	*tour*
le	**point de vue**	*vantage point, scenic overlook*

Nous allons faire une excursion.	*We're going on an outing.*
Le circuit des châteaux de la Loire.	*A tour of the Loire castles.*

b.

la	**mer**	*sea, ocean*
la	**Méditerranée**	*Mediterranean*
la	**côte**	*coast*
la	**grotte**	*cave*

l'	**île**	*island*
le	**lac**	*lake*
la	**rivière**	*river*
le	**bois**	*wood*
la	**forêt**	*forest*
le	**jardin**	*park, gardens*
le	**rocher**	*rock*
la	**montagne**	*mountain*

La Côte d'Azur.	*The French Riviera.*
Le jardin des Tuileries.	*The Tuileries Gardens.*
Le mont Blanc.	*Mont Blanc.*

c.

la	**plage**	*beach*
la	**piscine**	*swimming pool*
	nager	*to swim*
	bronzer	*to tan*
le	**voilier**	*sailing boat*
l'	**école de voile**	*sailing school*
la	**barque**	*boat*
le	**pédalo**	*pedal boat*
le	**ski nautique**	*water skiing*
la	**planche à voile**	*sail board*
la	**pêche**	*fishing*
le	**tennis**	*tennis*
la	**promenade**	*walk, stroll*
l'	**alpinisme**	*mountain-climbing*

La piscine chauffée.	*Heated pool.*
Je voudrais louer...	*I'd like to hire...*
Nous allons faire une promenade.	*We're going for a walk.*

d.

l'	**appareil photo**	*camera*
le	**film**	*film*
la	**pellicule**	*film*
le	**flash**	*flash*
la	**pile**	*battery*
la	**photo**	*photo*

Vous avez des films en couleurs?	*Do you have any colour film?*
Le flash ne marche pas.	*The flash isn't working.*

16 Excursions and Recreation

What can you see in these pictures? Answer in French, beginning **Je vois...** (*I see...*)

1

Mont Blanc

2

The French Riviera

3

The Tuileries Gardens

4   What sign do you look for if you want to go to:
    (*a*) the beach;
    (*b*) the swimming pool?

5   Say you would like to hire:
    (*a*) a pedal boat;
    (*b*) a sail board.

You would like to buy the following items. Ask for them
in French, beginning **Je voudrais acheter ...** (*I would like
to buy ...*)

6

7

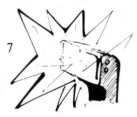

8

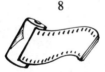

- The most popular **tourist areas** in France (apart from
  Paris) are: Normandy coast, Brittany, Atlantic coast,
  Côte d'Azur, Loire Valley, the Auvergne, Provence,
  Alsace, the Alps.
- **Beaches**   In most seaside resorts, beach clubs provide
  organised activities and games for children. Topless
  sunbathing is tolerated on most beaches, but naturism
  is restricted to certain beaches (especially numerous in
  the South of France).
- Some of the most popular **leisure activities** are fishing,
  hunting and horseracing. **Boules** or **pétanque** are
  played all over France, in the village square or street.
  The bowls are made of metal, and thrown rather than
  rolled.

17 The Weather

a. The Weather **b.** Good Weather
c. Bad Weather **d.** Cold Weather

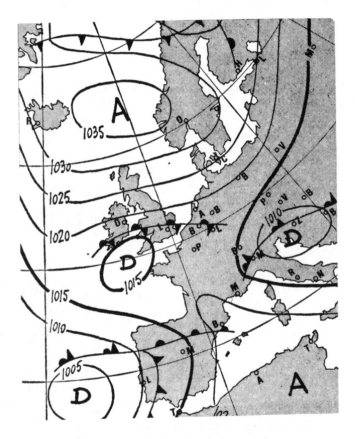

a.	la **météo**	*weather forecast*
	le **temps**	*weather*

Quel temps fera-t-il?	*What's the weather going to be like?*
Quel temps fait-il?	*What is the weather like?*

b.

le	**beau temps**	*good weather*
le	**soleil**	*sun*
la	**température**	*temperature*
	chaud	*warm, hot*
	Anticyclone (A)	*high-pressure area*

Il fait beau temps.	*The weather is good.*
Il fait chaud.	*It's warm/hot.*
Le soleil brille.	*The sun is shining.*
Il y a 25 degrés à l'ombre.	*It's 25 degrees (= 77° F) in the shade.*
L'eau est bonne.	*The water is warm. (= The water is good.)*

c.

	Dépression (D)	*low-pressure area*
le	**mauvais temps**	*bad weather*
le	**brouillard**	*fog*
le	**nuage**	*cloud*
	nuageux	*cloudy*
	couvert	*overcast*
la	**pluie**	*rain*
l'	**averse**	*shower*
la	**grêle**	*hail*
l'	**orage**	*thunderstorm*
le	**parapluie**	*umbrella*
le	**vent**	*wind*
la	**brume**	*mist*
l'	**éclaircie**	*clearing up*

Il fait mauvais temps.	*The weather is bad.*
Le ciel est couvert.	*The sky is overcast.*
Il pleut.	*It's raining.*
Il fait du vent.	*It is windy.*
Il fait de l'orage.	*It is stormy.*

d.

	froid	*cold*
le	**verglas**	*ice/icy roads*
la	**neige**	*snow*

Il fait froid.	*It's cold.*
Il neige.	*It's snowing.*

17 The Weather

Look at this weather map from **France-Soir**:

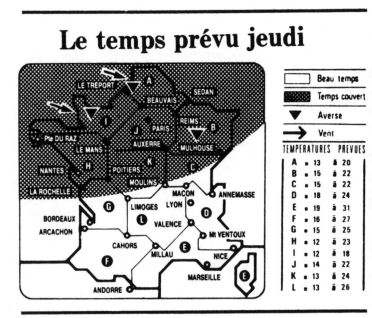

Le temps prévu jeudi

1 For which day is the weather forecast?

2 What is the weather like
   (a) in Paris?
   (b) in Le Tréport?
   (c) in Marseille?

3 What is the temperature
   (a) in Paris?
   (b) in Lyon?
   (c) in Nantes?

What is the weather like?

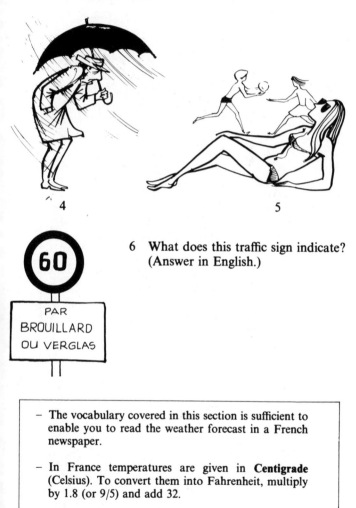

4

5

6 What does this traffic sign indicate?
(Answer in English.)

60

PAR
BROUILLARD
OU VERGLAS

- The vocabulary covered in this section is sufficient to enable you to read the weather forecast in a French newspaper.

- In France temperatures are given in **Centigrade** (Celsius). To convert them into Fahrenheit, multiply by 1.8 (or 9/5) and add 32.

Celsius	−5	0	5	10	15	20	25	30	35
Fahrenheit	23	32	41	50	59	68	77	86	95

18 Post Office and Telephone

a. Post Office **b.** Letters and Postcards
c. Telephone

a.

la	**poste**	*post office/post*
le	**bureau de poste (P.T.T.)**	*post office*
le	**guichet**	*counter*
la	**boîte aux lettres**	*letter-box*

Pardon, monsieur, où est la poste?	*Excuse me, where is the post office?*

b.

la	**lettre**	*letter*
la	**carte postale**	*postcard*
l'	**adresse**	*address*
le	**code postal**	*post code*
le	**timbre**	*stamp*
le	**télégramme**	*telegram*
le	**formulaire**	*form*
l'	**expéditeur**	*sender*
	par avion	*air mail*

Quel est le prix d'un timbre pour ... ?	*How much is a stamp for ... ?*
Un timbre pour une carte postale pour l'Angleterre, s.v.p.	*A stamp for a postcard to England, please.*
Cinq timbres à 2.30 F s.v.p.	*Five stamps at 2.30 F, please.*

c.

le	**téléphone**	*telephone*
le	**numeró de téléphone**	*telephone number*
l'	**indicatif**	*area code*
l'	**annuaire**	*telephone book*
la	**cabine téléphonique**	*telephone box*
le	**récepteur**	*receiver*
le	**standardiste**	*operator*
la	**communication en PCV**	*reverse charge call*

Quel est votre numéro de téléphone?	*What's your telephone number?*
Allô!	*Hello!*
C'est bien le 79-05-46?	*Is that 79-05-46?*
Ne quittez pas.	*Hold the line, please.*

18 Post Office and Telephone

What are these called in French?

6 You want to buy a stamp for a post card to Australia.
   What do you ask for?

7 How do you ask for three stamps at 3F each?

8 You would like someone's telephone number. What
   do you ask him?

9 You telephone someone. When he answers the phone,
   what does he say?

10   What is this called in French?

11   You are not sure if you have the right number. What
     do you say?

- **Post office** hours are 8 am to 7 pm on weekdays, 8 am
  to noon on Saturdays. Stamps can be bought at cafés,
  from a **café-tabac** or a stamp machine in the post
  office. French letter-boxes are usually yellow and have
  different slots for local deliveries and deliveries to other
  areas (*autres destinations*). Check also the time of
  collection, as in some areas this may be only once a day
  or even once a week.

- **Telephones**   There are fewer public phone boxes in
  France, and many calls are made from cafés or post
  offices. You can now dial direct to the UK from
  France. Dial 19, wait for the continuous tone, then dial
  44 followed by your STD code minus the first 0, and
  your number. You will need 5F, 1F and ½F coins. For
  local calls, *jetons* (tokens) can be bought at cafés. Most
  of the instructions in French phone boxes are translated into English. Emergency numbers are: Fire 18,
  Police 17, Operator 13, Directory Enquiries 12.

19   Clothing and Toiletries

a. Clothing **b.** Socks and Shoes **c.** Colours
d. Toiletries **e.** Hair Care

a.

les	**vêtements**	*clothes*
le	**pull-over**	*pullover, sweater*
la	**robe**	*dress*
la	**jupe**	*skirt*
la	**chemise**	*shirt*
la	**veste**	*jacket*
le	**pantalon**	*trousers*
la	**ceinture**	*belt*
le	**chapeau**	*hat*
le	**foulard**	*scarf*
les	**gants**	*gloves*
le	**manteau**	*coat*
l'	**imperméable**	*raincoat*
le	**maillot de bain**	*swimming costume*

Vêtements pour hommes.	*Men's wear.*
Vêtements pour dames.	*Women's wear.*
Je désire un pull-over.	*I'd like a pullover.*
Quelle est votre taille?	*What size?*
C'est trop grand/étroit.	*It's too big/tight.*
C'est trop court/long.	*It's too short/long.*
Avez-vous quelque chose	*Have you anything larger/*
de plus grand/petit?	*smaller?*

Je ne l'aime pas.	*I don't like it.*
C'est chic. C'est élégant.	*That's smart. That's elegant.*
Je le prends.	*I'll take it.*

b.

les **chaussures**	*shoes*
les **bas**	*stockings*
les **chaussettes**	*socks*
le **collant**	*tights*

Je désire	*I'd like*
une paire de chaussures.	*a pair of shoes.*
Quelle pointure faites-vous?	*What size do you take?*

c.

la **couleur**	*colour*
blanc, noir	*white, black*
gris	*grey*
rouge, vert	*red, green*
bleu, jaune	*blue, yellow*
marron	*chestnut brown*

d.

le **savon**	*soap*
le **shampooing**	*shampoo*
la **serviette de toilette**	*towel*
le **dentifrice**	*toothpaste*
la **brosse à dents**	*toothbrush*
le **rasoir électrique**	*electric razor*
l' **eau de Cologne**	*Cologne*
le **parfum**	*perfume*
la **serviette hygiénique**	*sanitary towel*
le **mouchoir**	*handkerchief*
l' **huile solaire**	*suntan oil*
les **lunettes**	*glasses*

| Les mouchoirs de papier. | *Paper tissues.* |
| Les lunettes de soleil. | *Sunglasses.* |

e.

| le **coiffeur** | *hairdresser/barber* |
| la **brosse**, le **peigne** | *brush, comb* |

| Une coupe, s.v.p. | *A haircut, please.* |
| Un shampooing mise en plis. | *A shampoo and set, please.* |

Money, Shopping→ 9

19 Clothing and Toiletries

1 What are these in French? Say you'd like to buy them.

(a)

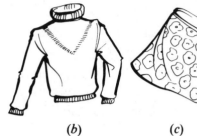

(b)

(c)

(d)

(e)

(f)

(g)

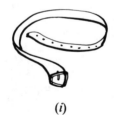

(h)

(i)

2 Say the pullover is too short.

3 Ask if the assistant has anything bigger.

4 Say you'll take it.

5 How does the assistant ask what size you take?

What are following called in French? Ask the chemist if
he has them.
Begin: **Est-ce que vous avez...**

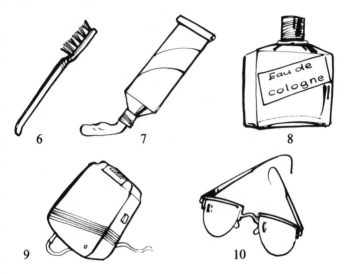

- When buying **clothes** or **shoes**, remember that French
  sizes are different from British ones.

Shoe sizes

British	1	2	3	4	5	6	7	8	9	10	11	12
French	33	34–35	36	37	38	39–40	41	42	43	44	45	46

Dress sizes

British	10	12	14	16	18	20
French	38	40	42	44	46	48

Collar sizes

British	13	13½	14	14½	15	15½	16	16½	17
French	33	34	35–36	37	38	39	41	42	43

Suits, coats

British	36	38	40	42	44	46
French	46	48	50	52	54	56

a. Breakdowns, Accidents **b.** Theft **c.** Police
d. Doctor **e.** Illness **f.** Chemist **g.** Help

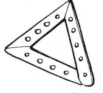

a.	la **panne**	*breakdown*
	le **service de dépannage**	*emergency breakdown service*
	le **garage**	*garage*
	l' **accident**	*accident*
	l' **accrochage**	*collision*
	l' **assurance**	*insurance*

Je suis en panne.	*My car has broken down.*
Téléphonez au service de dépannage.	*Call the breakdown service.*
Votre police d'assurance.	*Your insurance papers?*
Signaler un accident.	*To report an accident.*
Vous êtes coupable.	*It's your fault.*

b.		**oublier**	*forget*
		perdre	*lose*
		voler	*steal*
	le	**voleur**	*thief*
	le	**porte-monnaie**	*purse*
	le	**portefeuille**	*wallet*

J'ai perdu la clé.	*I've lost the key.*
Objets perdus.	*Lost property.*
On m'a volé mon argent.	*Somebody's stolen my money.*

c.	la **police**	*police*
	la **gendarmerie**	*police (in the country)*
	la **contravention**	*offence*
	l' **avocat**	*lawyer*

Appelez la police!	*Call the police!*
Un agent de police.	*Policeman.*

d.

le	**médecin**	*doctor*
le	**dentiste**	*dentist*
l'	**ambulance**	*ambulance*
l'	**hôpital**	*hospital*
les	**premiers secours**	*first aid*

Vite, un médecin!	*Get a doctor, quick!*
Ce n'est pas grave.	*It's nothing serious.*

e.

	malade	*ill*
le	**coup de soleil**	*sunburn*
le	**rhume**	*cold*
l'	**indigestion**	*indigestion*
la	**crise cardiaque**	*heart attack*

Je suis malade.	*I'm ill.*
J'ai mal à la tête.	*I have a headache.*
J'ai mal au ventre.	*I have stomach-ache.*
J'ai de la fièvre.	*I have a fever.*
Je suis blessé.	*I'm hurt/injured.*
Je me suis brûlé la main.	*I have burnt my hand.*
Je me suis coupé le doigt.	*I have cut my finger.*
J'ai mal aux dents.	*I have toothache.*

f.

la	**pharmacie**	*chemist, pharmacy*
le	**médicament**	*medicine*
la	**pommade**	*ointment*
le	**comprimé**	*tablet*
le	**somnifère**	*sleeping pill*
le	**tricostéril**	*bandage*
le	**sparadrap**	*sticking plaster*

La pharmacie de service.	*Chemist on emergency duty. (open 24 hours)*
Du tricostéril, s.v.p.	*Some bandages, please.*

g.

	Attention	*Caution*
le	**secours**	*help*

Au secours!	*Help!*
Sortie de secours.	*Emergency Exit.*

20 Accidents and Emergencies

1 You telephone a garage. Tell the mechanic that your car has broken down.

2 You are involved in an accident. How do you ask someone to call the police?

3 Say you would like to report an accident.

4 You were to blame for the accident. What do the police say to you?

5 Tell the police you have lost your wallet.

6 Say that someone has stolen your camera.

7 You have witnessed an accident. How do you ask someone to call an ambulance?

8 You are not feeling well and go to the doctor. Tell him you have
(*a*) a headache; (*b*) a cold; (*c*) burnt your finger; (*d*) cut your foot. (**le pied**)

9 The doctor does not think it is serious. What does he say?

10 Ask the chemist for
(*a*) some ointment; (*b*) a bottle of sleeping pills; (*c*) some sticking plasters.

11 Tell the dentist you have toothache.

12 You are locked inside a building. What do you shout through the window?

13 The main exit is blocked. What sign do you look for?

- Drivers caught breaking the **speed limit** or **drink/driving limit** (which is the same as in the UK, and for which there are random breath tests) may be fined on the spot and must pay in cash. A receipt will be given.

- There are **emergency telephones** every 2 km on motorways and there is a **24-hour garage** approximately every 20 km. Emergency phone numbers are: Fire 18, Police 17, Operator 13, Directory Enquiries 12.

- There is a reciprocal agreement over **Health Cover** between France and the UK, and if you are eligible, you can recover about 80 % of doctors' or hospital bills. Form E111 should be obtained *in advance*. However, it is advisable to take out adequate insurance, as a visit to a doctor is expensive and the bill must be settled immediately.

- **Chemists** First aid, medical advice and a night service rota are available from **pharmacies**, which can be recognised by their green cross. The address of the nearest **pharmacie** can be obtained from the **gendarmerie.**

- In order to say that you are ill, use the following expression:
    J'ai mal à la . . . (for feminine nouns)
            au . . . (for masculine nouns)
          aux . . . (for nouns in the plural)

The main **parts of the body** are:

la	**tête**	*head*	la	**main** *hand*
les	**yeux**	*eyes*	le	**doigt** *finger*
le	**nez**	*nose*	le	**coude** *elbow*
les	**oreilles**	*ears*	la	**jambe** *leg*
la	**bouche**	*mouth*	le	**pied** *foot*
le	**cou**	*neck*	le	**doigt de pied** *toe*
la	**gorge**	*throat*	le	**genou** *knee*
le	**bras**	*arm*	la	**dent** *tooth*

Answers

1 General Expressions
1 Oui, madame. 2 Non, monsieur. 3 Oui, monsieur.
4 Non, madame. 5 Bonjour, monsieur. 6 Bonjour,
madame. 7 Au revoir, monsieur. 8 Votre passeport, s.v.p.
9 Merci, monsieur. 10 Pardon, madame. 11 Voici mon
mari. 12 Voici ma femme.

2 Arriving in France
1 La valise (une valise). 2 Le sac (un sac). 3 Avez-vous
quelque chose à déclarer? 4 Non, monsieur, rien à déclarer.
5 Ouvrez le coffre. 6. Ouvrez la valise. 7 Je
m'appelle . . . 8 Votre passeport, s.v.p. 9 Votre permis de
conduire, s.v.p. 10 Je ne comprends pas. 11 Oui, je suis
Anglais. 12 Vous pouvez passer. 13 La Grande Bretagne.
14 L'Australie. 15 La France. 16 Vous avez un journal
anglais?

3 Driving a Car
1 La voiture (une voiture). 2 Le camion (un camion).
3 Super? Ordinaire? 4 Faites le plein, s.v.p. 5 Vérifiez
l'huile et les pneus, s.v.p. 6 Bonne route! 7 Autoroute.
8 Route Nationale 20. 9 Parking. 10 Stationnement
interdit. 11 Une station-service.

4 Finding Your Way
1 nord, sud, est, ouest. 2 Un plan de Paris, s.v.p. 3 Vous
avez une carte routière? 4 Où est la Place de la Concorde,
s.v.p.? 5 Tournez à droite. 6 Tournez à gauche. 7 Allez
tout droit. 8 C'est loin? 9 Attendez. 11 Allez à gauche.

5 Public Transport
1 Information/Renseignements. 2 Consigne. 3 Trains de
banlieue. 4 Grandes lignes. 5 Un billet aller et retour pour
Paris, s.v.p. 6 Wagon-restaurant. 7 Wagon-lit *ou*
Couchettes. 8 À l'aéroport, s.v.p. 9 Départ.
10 Correspondance. 11 Sortie. 12 Un carnet, s.v.p.

6 Accommodation
1 Le lit. 2 La clé. 3 Je cherche un bon hôtel. 4 Vous
avez une chambre libre? 5 Une chambre avec douche pour une
nuit, s.v.p. 6 Quel est le prix avec petit déjeuner? 7 C'est
trop cher. 8 La note. 9 Le rez-de-chaussée 10 Où sont
les toilettes? 11 Libre. 12 Occupé.

7 Numbers, Weights and Measures

1 Quinze. 2 Dix-sept. 3 Cent dix. 4 Deux cent douze. 5 Voie numéro cinq. 6 Huit. 7 Deux. 8 Un. 9 Trois. 10 (*a*) Quatre-vingt-dix kilomètres; (*b*) deux cent vingt km; (*c*) quatre cent soixante km; (*d*) sept cent quatre-vingts km; (*e*) cinq cent soixante km; (*f*) cinq cent quatre-vingts km. 11 Trente-trois, rue de Verdun, soixante-quinze zéro quarante-six Paris. 12 Deux cent cinquante grammes. 13 Un kilo de cafe. 14 Un kilo de tomates, s.v.p.

8 Times and Dates

1 Quelle heure est-il? 2 (*a*) il est neuf heures du matin; (*b*) il est six heures et demie; (*c*) il est sept heures et quart. 3 (*a*) il est trois heures de l'après-midi (quinze heures); (*b*) il est quatre heures moins le quart de l'après-midi (seize heures moins le quart); (*c*) il est sept heures du soir (dix-neuf heures). 4 (*a*) vingt minutes; (*b*) une demi-heure; (*c*) dix jours; (*d*) six mois. 5 (Je pars) à minuit. 6 À quelle heure part le train? 7 De dix heures et demie à dix-huit heures et demie, et de dix-huit heures et demie à vingt-trois heures. 8 Vendredi le vingt-deux août.

9 Money and Shopping

1 Bureau de change. 2 Que désirez-vous? 3 Vous avez des pull-overs? 4 C'est combien (, la chemise)? 5 C'est 150 francs. 6 Et avec ça? 7 Vous payez à la caisse. 8 Ça fait combien? 9 (*a*) dix francs cinquante; (*b*) neuf francs cinquante; (*c*) vingt francs. 10 (*a*) trois cent vingt-cinq francs; (*b*) deux cent trente-neuf francs; (*c*) deux cent dix-neuf francs.

10 Meals

1 Le petit déjeuner, le déjeuner et le dîner. 2 (*a*) la fourchette; (*b*) l'assiette; (*c*) le couteau; (*d*) la cuiller; (*e*) le verre; (*f*) la bouteille. 3 (*a*) la baguette; (*b*) le croissant; (*c*) le beurre. 4 Un verre de vin, s.v.p. 5 Une baguette, s.v.p. 6 Un café au lait, s.v.p. 7 Une omelette au jambon, s.v.p. 8 Un sandwich au fromage, s.v.p.

11 Restaurants

1 (*a*) un restaurant; (*b*) un café *ou* un bar; (*c*) un salon de thé. 2 (*a*) la chaise; (*b*) la table. 3 Avez-vous une table pour deux personnes? 4 La carte et la carte des vins, s.v.p. 5 Je prends le menu numéro un. 6 Et comme boisson? 7 Garçon! L'huile et le vinaigre, s.v.p. 8 Apportez-moi l'addition, s.v.p. 9 (*a*) le plateau de fromage; (*b*) le sel; (*c*) le poivre.

Answers

12 Starters, Meat, Fish
1 La côtelette, s.v.p.   2 Le poulet rôti, s.v.p.   3 Le poisson,
s.v.p.   4 Les crevettes, s.v.p.   5 Le potage bonne femme,
s.v.p. *ou* Je prends le potage bonne femme.   6 Le pâté, s.v.p.
7 L'escalope, s.v.p.   8 Un steak bien cuit, s.v.p.   9 Un steak
saignant, s.v.p.   10 Les œufs sur le plat, s.v.p.   11 La
bouillabaisse, s.v.p.   12 Cheese, white bread, white wine,
pepper, salt, bouillon.

13 Vegetables, Fruit, Desserts
1 Les haricots verts. J'aime les haricots verts.   2 Les oignons.
J'aime les oignons.   3 Les carottes. J'aime les carottes.   4 Les
pommes de terre. J'aime les pommes de terre.   5 Les artichauts.
J'aime les artichauts.   6 Les champignons. J'aime les
champignons.   7 Les cerises. J'aime les cerises.   8 Les raisins.
J'aime les raisins.   9 Les fraises. J'aime les fraises.   10 Les
oranges. J'aime les oranges.   11 Les bananes. J'aime les
bananes.   12 Le melon. J'aime le melon.   13 Des tomates
farcies, s.v.p.   14 (Apportez-moi) la crème, s.v.p.
15 Glaces.   16 Vanille et chocolat.

14 Drinking and Smoking
1 Café ou thé?   2 Un café crème, s.v.p.   3 Un paquet de
cigarettes et une boîte d'allumettes, s.v.p.   4 Vous fumez une
cigarette?   5 Des cigarettes (Un paquet de cigarettes).   6 Des
allumettes (Une boîte d'allumettes).   7 Un briquet.   8 Un
cendrier.   9 Une bouteille.   10 Un ouvre-bouteilles.   11 Je
voudrais un jus de pommes.   12 Je voudrais une bouteille de vin
rouge.   13 Je voudrais une bière blonde.   14 Je voudrais un
verre de cognac.

15 Sightseeing and Entertainment
1 L'Arc de Triomphe.   2 La Tour Eiffel.   3 Le Château de
Versailles.   4 La Vénus de Milo.   5 Le syndicat d'initiative.
6 À quelle heure commence le spectacle?   7 (Il commence) à
sept heures/dix-neuf heures.   8 Heures d'Ouverture.
9 Caisse.   10 Entrée.   11 Sortie.   12 Fermé.

16 Excursions and Recreation
1 Je vois le mont Blanc.   2 Je vois la Côte d'Azur.   3 Je
vois le jardin des Tuileries.   4 (*a*) Plage; (*b*) Piscine.   5 Je
voudrais louer (*a*) un pédalo; (*b*) une planche à voile.   6 Je
voudrais acheter un appareil photo.   7 Je voudrais acheter un
flash.   8 Je voudrais acheter une pellicule.

Answers

17 The Weather

1 Jeudi. 2 (a) le ciel est couvert; (b) il pleut et il fait du vent; (c) il fait beau temps. 3 (a) 14° à 22°; (b) 15° à 22°; (c) 12° à 23°. 4 Il fait du vent/Il fait froid. 5 Il fait chaud/Le soleil brille. 6 A maximum speed limit of 60 km/h applies in fog or ice.

18 Post Office and Telephone

1 Des/les cartes postales. 2 Une boîte aux lettres. 3 Une lettre. 4 Un timbre. 5 L'adresse. 6 Un timbre pour une carte postale pour l'Australie, s.v.p. 7 Trois timbres à trois francs, s.v.p. 8 Quel est votre numéro de téléphone? 9 Âllo! 10 Le téléphone. 11 C'est bien le . . . ?

19 Clothing and Toiletries

1 Je voudrais acheter *ou* Je désire . . . (a) une robe; (b) un pull-over; (c) une jupe; (d) une veste; (e) un pantalon; (f) une chemise; (g) un chapeau; (h) un maillot de bain; (i) une ceinture. 2 Le pull-over est trop court. 3 Avez-vous quelque chose de plus grand? 4 Je le prends. (Je **la** prends *if the object is feminine*.) 5 Quelle est votre taille? *ou* Quelle pointure faites-vous? (*shoes*) 6 Est-ce que vous avez une brosse à dents? 7 Est-ce que vous avez du dentifrice (un tube de dentifrice)? 8 Est-ce que vous avez de l'eau de Cologne? 9 Est-ce que vous avez un rasoir électrique? 10 Est-ce que vous avez des lunettes de soleil?

20 Accidents and Emergencies

1 Je suis en panne. 2 Appelez la police! 3 Je voudrais signaler un accident. 4 Vous êtes coupable. 5 J'ai perdu mon portefeuille. 6 On m'a volé mon appareil. 7 Appelez une ambulance! *ou* Vite, une ambulance! 8 (a) j'ai mal à la tète; (b) j'ai un rhume (un grand rhume = a heavy cold); (c) je me suis brûlé le doigt; (d) je me suis coupé le pied. 9 Ce n'est pas grave. 10 (a) (Donnez-moi) de la pommade, s.v.p.; (b) une bouteille de somnifères, s.v.p.; (c) du sparadrap, s.v.p. 11 J'ai mal aux dents. 12 Au secours! 13 Sortie de secours.

French-English Vocabulary

accident accident 20a
accrochage collision 20a
acheter buy 9c
addition bill 11d
aéroport airport 5b
agence de voyages travel agency 15a
agent de police policeman 20c
agneau lamb 12b
ail garlic 13a
alimentation grocer's 9
aller go drive 3a
allez walk 4c; go (feel) 1c
allô hello 18c
allumette match 14c
alpinisme mountain-climbing 16c
ambassade embassy 2c
ambulance ambulance 20d
anglais English 2c
Anglais English (man) 2c
Anglaise English (woman) 2c
Angleterre England 2c
annuaire telephone book 18c
anticyclone high-pressure area 17b
août August 8c
à point medium 12b
appareil photo camera 16d
apportez bring 11d
après-midi afternoon 8b/8a
argent money 9a
arrêt d'autobus bus stop 5d
arrivée arrival 5e
artichaut artichoke 13a
ascenseur lift 6b
assiette plate, dish 10b
assurance insurance 20a
attendez stop (wait) 4c
attention caution 3b/20g
auberge de la jeunesse youth hostel 6a
aujourd'hui today 8b
au revoir goodbye 1b
Australie Australia 2c
Australien/ne Austalian 2c
autobus 5d
autoroute motorway 3b
avec with 6b/14c
avenue avenue 4c

averse shower 17c
avion aeroplane 5b
avocat lawyer 20c

bagages luggage 2a
baguette French bread 10c
banque bank 9b
bar bar 11a
barque boat 16c
bas stockings 19b
bateau boat, ship 5c
beau good 17b
beaucoup very much 1c; a lot 7b
belge Belgian 2c
Belgique Belgium 2c
beurre butter 7c/10c
bien well 1b/2a
bien cuit well-done 12b
bière beer 14b
bifteck beefsteak 12b
billet ticket 5a/15d
blanc white 19c
blessé hurt, injured 20e
bleu blue 19c
bœuf beef 12b
boire drink 10a
bois wood 16b
boissons drinks 14a
boîte box 14c
boîte aux lettres letter-box 18a
boîte de nuit night club 15c
bol bowl 10b
bon good 6a
bonbon sweet 13c
bonjour good morning, good afternoon, hello 1b
bon marché cheap 9d
boucherie butcher's shop 9
boulangerie bakery 9
boulevard boulevard 4c
bouteille bottle 10b/14b
briquet lighter 14c
bronzer tan 16c
brosse brush 19e
brosse à dents toothbrush 19d
brouillard fog 17c
brume mist 17c

bureau de change currency exchange 9b
bureau de poste post office 18a
bureau de tabac tobacconist 14c

cabillaud cod 12c
cabine téléphonique telephone box 18c
café coffee 10c/11c/14a; café, bar 11a
caisse cash desk 9d; ticket window 15d
camion lorry 3a
car bus, coach 5d
carafe jug 10b
caravane caravan 3a
carnet book of tickets 5d
carte map 4a, menu 11b
carte de crédit credit card 9b
carte des vins wine list 11b
carte grise car registration papers 2b
carte postale postcard 18b
caverne cave 16b
ce this 1e
ceinture belt 19a
cendrier ashtray 14c
centre ville city centre 4b
cerise cherry 13b
c'est it is 1e
cette this 1e
chaise chair 11a
chambre room 6b
champagne champagne 14b
champignon mushroom 13a
changer change, exchange 9b
chapeau hat 19a
chateau castle, palace 15b/16a
chaud warm, hot 17b
chaussettes socks 19b
chaussures shoes 19b
chemins de fer railways 5a
chemise shirt 9c/19a
chèque de voyage traveller's cheque 9b
cher expensive 6c/9d
chic smart 19a

chocolat chocolate 13c; cocoa, hot chocolate 10c
chou cabbage 13a
choux de Bruxelles Brussels sprouts 13a
cidre cider 14b
ciel sky 17c
cinéma cinema 15c
circuit tour 16a
circulation traffic 3a
citron lemon 10c/13b/14a
clé key 1f/6b/20b
code postal post code 18b
coffre boot 2a
coiffeur hairdresser, barber 19e
collant tights 19b
combien how much 3c/6c/9d; how many 7b/11a
commander order 11b
commencer begin 15c
comment how 1b
complet fully booked 6b
comprendre understand 2c
comprimé tablet 20f
confiture jam, marmalade 10c
consigne left luggage 5a
consigne automatique lockers 5a
consommé clear soup, consommé 12a
contravention offence 20c
correspondance connection 5d
côte coast 16b
côtelette chop 12b
couchettes couchettes, Pullman 5a
couleur colour 19c
coup de soleil sunburn 20e
coupe haircut 19e
coupé cut 20e
court short 19a
couteau knife 10b
couvert overcast 17c
crème cream 13c
crêpe crêpe, pancake 10d/12c
crevettes shrimps 12d
crise cardiaque heart attack 20e
croque-monsieur toasted sandwich 10d
crudités raw vegetable salad 12a

French-English Vocabulary

cuiller spoon 10b
curiosités sights 15b

dames ladies 6d
danger danger 3b
déclarer declare 2a
degré degree 17b
déjeuner lunch 10a
demain tomorrow 8b
demi half 8a
demi-bouteille half-bottle 14b
demi-heure half an hour 8a
demi-pension room with breakfast
   and one main meal included 6c
dentifrice toothpaste 19d
dentiste dentist 20d
dents teeth 20e
départ departure 5e
dépression low-pressure area 17c
dessert dessert 11b
déviation diversion 3b
dimanche Sunday 8c
dîner dinner, supper 10a
direction direction 4d
disque parking disc 3d
doigt finger 20e
domicile place of residence 2b
douane customs 2a
douche shower 6b
droite right 4d

eau water 10b/17b
eau de Cologne Cologne 19d
éclaircie clearing up 17c
école de voile sailing school 16c
Ecossais Scottish 2c
Ecosse Scotland 2c
église church 15b
embarcadère embarkment area 5c
encaisser cash 9b
entrecôte rib steak 12b
entrée entrance 15d
épicerie grocer's 9
escalier stairs 6b
escalope veal cutlet 12b
escargots snails 12b
essence petrol 3c
est east 4d

et and 6b
étage floor, storey 6b
étroit tight 19a
excursion excursion, outing 16a
expéditeur sender 18b
express express train 5a

femme woman 1d; wife 1f
fermé closed 8c/15d
fête festival 15c
feu rouge traffic light 4c
fièvre fever 20e
fille girl 1d
filtre filtre 1£
flash flash 16d
forêt forest 16b
formulaire form 18b
foulard scarf 19a
fourchette fork 10b
fraise strawberry 10c/13b
framboises raspberries 13b
français French 2c
Français Frenchman 2c
Française Frenchwoman 2c
France France 2c
frites chips 10a/13a
froid cold 17d
fromage cheese 10d/11b
fruits fruit 10c/13b
fruits de mer shellfish 12d
fumer smoke 14c

Gallois Welsh 2c
gant glove 19a
garage garage 3d/20a
garçon boy 1d; waiter 11d
gare station 5a
gasoil diesel 3c
gâteau cake 13c
gauche left 4d
gendarmerie police 20c
gibier game 12b
gigot leg of lamb 12b
glace ice cream 13c
glacé iced 13b
goûter tea 10a
grand big 19a

French-English Vocabulary

grandes lignes main lines, long-distance trains 5a
grand magasin department store 9c
gratuit free 9d
grave serious 20f
gravillons gravel 4
grêle hail 17c
grenouilles frogs 12b
gris grey 19c
guichet ticket office 5a; counter 18a
guide guide 15d

haricots verts runner beans 13a
heure hour, o'clock 8a
heures d'ouverture opening hours 15d
hier yesterday 8b
homme man 1d
hôpital hospital 20d
horaire timetable 5e
horloge clock 8a
hors d'œuvre appetizer, hors d'œuvre 11b
hôtel de ville town hall 4b
huile oil 3c/11c
huile solaire suntan oil 19d
huîtres oysters 12d

île island 16b
imperméable raincoat 19a
indicatif area code 18c
indigestion indigestion 20e

jambon ham 10d
jardin park, gardens 16b
jaune yellow 19c
je I 1f
jeudi Thursday 8c
jour day 8b
journal newspaper 2c
juillet July 8c
jupe skirt 19a
jus juice 10c/14a
jusqu'à to 7b

la the 1e
là-bas over there 6d
lac lake 16b

lait milk 7b/10c/14a
le the 1e
légumes vegetables 13a
les the 1e
lettre letter 18b
libre free 5d/6b/11a, vacant 6d
libre-service self-service 9c
liqueur liqueur 14b
lit bed 6b
livre pound 9b
location de voitures car rental 3a
loin far 4d
long long 19a
louer hire 16c
lundi Monday 8c
lunettes glasses 19d

ma my 1f
madame madam 1a, Mrs 1d
mademoiselle Miss 1d/11d
magasin shop 9c
maillot de bain swimming costume 19a
main hand 20e
maintenant now 6c
maison house 4b
mal à la tête headache 20e
malade ill 20e
manger eat 10a/11a
manteau coat 19a
maquereau mackerel 12d
marché market 9c
mardi Tuesday 8c
mari husband 1f
marron chestnut brown 19c
matin morning 8a/8b
mauvais bad 17c
médecin doctor 20d
médicament medicine 20f
Méditerranée Mediterranean 16b
menu set meal, fixed-price meal 11b
mer sea 16b
merci thank you 1c/9c
mercredi Wednesday 8c
messieurs gentlemen 6d
météo weather forecast 17a
métro underground 5d
midi noon 8b

French-English Vocabulary

minuit midnight 8b
  mois month 8c
mon my 1f
monnaie small change 9a
monsieur gentleman, Mr 1d
montagne mountain 16b
montre watch 8a
mouchoir handkerchief 19d
moules mussels 12d
musée museum 15b

nager swim 16c
nappe tablecloth 10b
nationalité nationality 2c
neige snow 17d
noir black 19c
nom name 1f/2b
non no 1a/2a
nord north 4d
note bill 6c
nuage cloud 17c
nuageux cloudy 17c
nuit night 6b/8b
numéro de chambre room number 6b
numéro de téléphone telephone number 18c

obligatoire obligatory 3d
occupé engaged 6d
œuf egg 12c
oignon onion 12a/13a
ombre shade 17b
orage thunderstorm 17c
orange orange 13b
orangeade orange juice 14a
ordinaire regular 3c
ou or 14c
où where 4c/4d/5d/6a/15a/18a
oublier forget 20b
ouest west 4d
oui yes 1a/2a
ouvert open 15d
ouvre-bouteilles bottle opener 14b

pain bread 10c
paire de chaussures pair of shoes 19b

palais palace 15b
panne breakdown 20a
pantalon trousers 19a
paquet de cigarettes packet of cigarettes 14c
parapluie umbrella 17c
parking parking, car park 3d
passeport passport 2b
passer go on 2a
pâté de foie liver pâté 12b
pâtisserie cake shop 9; pastry 13c
payer pay 6c/9d
pays de Galles Wales 2c
péage road toll 3b
pêche fishing 16c
pédalo pedal boat 16c
peigne comb 19e
pèlerinage piligrimage 15b
pellicule film 16d
pension complète room with all meals included 6c
pension de famille guest house 6a
perdre lose 20b
permis de conduire driving licence 2b
petit déjeuner breakfast 6c/10a
petit pain bread roll 10c
peu a little 7b
pharmacie chemist's, pharmacy 20f
pièce coin 9a
pile battery 16d
piscine swimming pool 16c
place square 4c
plage beach 16c
plan street map 4a
planche de voile sailboard 16c
plat course, dish 11b
plateau de fromage cheese platter 11b
pluie rain 17c
pneus tyres 3c
poids lourds heavy vehicles 3a
point de vue vantage point 16a
pointure size 19b
poire pear 13b
pois peas 13a
poisson fish 12d
poivre pepper 11c

French-English Vocabulary

police police 20c
pommade ointment 20f
pomme apple 13b
pommes de terre potatoes 13a
pont bridge 4c; desk 5c
porc pork 12b
port port 5c
porte-monnaie purse 20b
portefeuille wallet 20b
potage soup 12a
poulet chicken 12c
pour for 6b/18b
pourboire tip 11d
poussez push 15d
premiers secours first aid 20d
prendre take 19a
prénom first name 2b
priorité right of way 3b
prix price 6c/9d
promenade walk, stroll 16c
prospectus brochure 15a
pull-over pullover, sweater 19a

quai embankment 4c
quand when 8b
quart d'heure quarter of an hour 8a
quelque chose anything 2a

ragoût stew 12b
raisin grape 13b
ralentir slow down 3b
rapide high-speed express train 5a
rasoir électrique electric razor 19d
récepteur receiver 18c
réception reception desk 6b
renseignements enquiries 5e
repas meal 10a
R.E.R. rapid transit 5d
réservation reservation 5a
réserver reserve 6b
retard delay 5e
rez-de-chaussée ground floor 6b
rhume cold 20e
rivière river 16b
riz rice 13a
robe dress 19a
rocher rock 16b
rôti roast 12c

rouge red 19c
route road 3b
rue street 4c/4d

sac handbag 2a
saignant rare 12b
salade lettuce 13a
salle à manger dining room 10a
salle d'attente waiting room 5a
salle de bains bathroom 6b
salle de concert concert hall 15c
salon de thé café, tea shop 11a
salut hello 1b
samedi Saturday 8c
sans without 14c
sauce sauce, gravy 12b
saucisse sausage 10d
savon soap 19d
secours help 20g
sel salt 11c
semaine week 8c
sens unique one-way street 4c
service service 11d
service de dépannage breakdown
  service 20a
serviette napkin 10b
serviette de toilette towel 19d
serviette hygiénique sanitary towel
  19d
shampooing shampoo 19d
signaler report 20a
s'il vous plaît please 1c
ski nautique water skiing 16c
soir evening 8a/8b
sole sole 12d
soleil sun 17b
somnifère sleeping pill 20f
sortie exit 5d/15d
sortie de secours emergency exit
  15d
soupe soup 12a
souper supper 10a
soupière soup bowl 10b
sparadrap plaster 20f
spectacle performance 15c
stade stadium 15c
station de métro underground station 5d

French-English Vocabulary

stationnement parking 3d
station-service service station 3c
sucre sugar 11c/13b
sud south 4d
Suisse Switzerland 2c
supermarché supermarket 9c
surveillé guarded 3d
syndicat d'initiative tourist information office 15a

table table 11a
taille size 19a
tarte tart 13c
tasse cup 10b
temps weather 17a
terrain de caiping camp site 6a
thé tea 10c/14a
timbre stamp 18b
tire-bouchon cork screw 14b
tirez pull 15d
toilettes toilets 6d
tour tower 15b
tour de ville sightseeing tour 4b
tournez turn 4d
tout droit straight ahead 4d
tout près near 4d
tous les jours everyday 8b
train train 5a
trains de banlieue local trains 5a
travaux road works 3b
tricostéril bandage 20f

un a, an 1e

valise suitcase 1e/1f

veau veal 12b
vendredi Friday 8c
vent wind 17c
ventre stomach 20a
verglas ice, icy roads 17d
vérifiez check 3c
verre glass 10b
vert green 19c
veste jacket 19a
vêtements clothes 19a
viande meat 12b
village village 4b
ville town 4b
vin wine 10b/14b
vinaigre vinegar 11c
virage bend 4d
visiter visit, see, tour 15b/15d
vite quick 20f
voici here's, here are 1e/11b
voie track, platform 5a
voilà there's, there are 1e/11a
voilier sailing boat 16c
voiture car 3a
vol flight 5b
voler steal 20b
voleur thief 20b
votre your 1f
vous you 1b/1f
voyage organisé conducted tour 15d

wagon-lit sleeping car 5a
wagon-restaurant dining car 5a

zone bleue limited parking 3d

English-French Vocabulary

a un 1e
accident accident 20a
aeroplane avion 5b
afternoon après-midi 8a/8b
airport aéroport 5b
a little peu 7b
a lot beaucoup 7b
ambulance ambulance 20d
an un 1e
and et 6b
anything quelque chose 2a
appetizer hors d'œuvre 11b
apple pomme 13b
area code indicatif 18c
arrival arrivée 5e
artichoke artichaut 13a
ashtray cendrier 14c
August août 8c
Australia Australie 2c
Australian Australien/ne 2c
avenue avenue 4c

bad mauvais 17c
bakery boulangerie 9
banana banane 13b
bandage tricostéril 20f
bank banque 9b
bar bar, café 11a
barber coiffeur 19e
bathroom salle de bains 6b
battery pile 16d
beach plage 16c
bed lit 6b
beef bœuf 12b
beefsteak bifteck 12b
beer bière 14b
begin commencer 15c
Belgian belge 2c
Belgium Belgique 2c
belt ceinture 19a
bend virage 4d
big grand 19a
bill note 6c; addition 11d
black noir 19c
blue bleu 19c
boat bateau 5c, barque 16c
boot coffre 2a
bottle bouteille 10b/14b

bottle opener ouvre-bouteilles 14b
boulevard boulevard 4c
bowl bol 10b
box boîte 14c
boy garçon 1d
bread pain 10c
bread roll petit pain 10c
breakdown panne 20a
breakdown service service de dépannage 20a
breakfast petit déjeuner 6c/10a
bridge pont 4c
bring apportez 11d
brochure prospectus 15a
brush brosse 19e
Brussels sprouts chou de Bruxelles 13a
bus autobus 5d
bus stop arrêt d'autobus 5d
butcher's boucherie 9
butter beurre 7c/10c
buy acheter 9c

cabbage chou 13a
cabin cabine 5c
café café, salon de thé 11a
cake gâteau 13c
cake shop pâtisserie 9
camera appareil photo 16d
camp site terrain de camping 6a
car voiture 3a
caravan caravane 3a
car registration papers carte grise 2b
car rental location de voitures 3a
cash encaisser 9b
cashier caisse 9d
cash register caisse 9d
castle château 15b/16a
caution attention 3b/20g
cave grotte 16b
chair chaise 11a
champagne champagne 14b
change changer 9b
cheap bon marché 9d
cheese fromage 10d/11b
cheese platter plateau de fromage 11b

English-French Vocabulary

chemist's pharmacie 20f
cherry cerise 13b
chestnut brown marron 19c
chicken poulet 12c
chips frites 10a/13a
chocolate chocolat 13c
chop côtelette 12b
church église 15b
cider cidre 14b
cinema cinéma 15c
city centre centre ville 4b
clearing up éclaircie 17c
clock horloge 8a
closed fermé 8c/15d
clothes vêtements 19a
cloud nuage 17c
cloudy nuageux 17c
coach car 5d
coast côte 16b
coat manteau 19a
cocoa chocolat 10c
cod cabillaud 12c
coffee café 10c/11c/14a
coin pièce 9a
cold froid 17d, rhume 20e
collision accrochage 20a
Cologne eau de Cologne 19d
colour couleur 19c
comb peigne 19e
concert hall salle de concert 15c
connection correspondance 5d
consulate consulat 2c
cork screw tire-bouchon 14b
counter guichet 18a
course plat 11b
cream crème 13c
credit card carte de crédit 9b
cup tasse 10b
currency exchange bureau de change 9b
customs douane 2a
cut coupé 20e

danger danger 3b
day jour 8b
deck pont 5c
declare déclarer 2a
degree degré 17b

delay retard 5e
dentist dentiste 20d
department store grand magasin 9c
departure départ 5e
dessert dessert 11b
diesel gasoil 3c
dining car wagon-restaurant 5a
dining room salle à manger 10a
dinner dîner 10a
direction direction 4d
dish assiette 10b, plat 11b
diversion déviation 3b
doctor médecin 20d
dress robe 19a
drink boire 10a
drinks boissons 14a
drive aller 3a
driving licence permis de conduire 2b

east est 4d
eat manager 10a/11a
egg œuf 12c
electric razor rasoir électrique 19d
embankment quai 4c
embarkment area embarcadère 5c
embassy ambassade 2c
emergency exit sortie de secours 15d
engaged occupé 6d
England Angleterre
English anglais
English(man) Anglais
English(woman) Anglaise
enquiries renseignements 5e
entrance entrée 15d
evening soir 8a/8b
every day tous les jours 8b
exchange changer 9b
excursion excursion 16a
exit sortie 5d/15d
expensive cher 6c/9d
express train express 5a

far loin 4d
festival fête 15c
fever fièvre 20e
film pellicule 16d

English-French Vocabulary

filter filtre 14c
finger doigt 20e
first aid premiers secours 20d
first name prénom 2b
fish poisson 12d
fishing pêche 16c
flash flash 16d
flight vol 5b
floor étage 6b
fog brouillard 17c
food alimentation 9
for pour 6b/18b
forest forêt 16b
forget oublier 20b
fork fourchette 10b
form formulaire 18b
France France 2c
free libre 5d/6b/11a, gratuit 9d
French français 2c
French bread baguette 10c
Frenchman Français 2c
Frenchwoman Française 2c
Friday vendredi 8c
frogs grenouilles 12b
fruit fruits 10c/13b
fully booked complet 6b

game gibier 12b
garage garage 3d/20a
garlic ail 13a
gentleman monsieur 1d
girl fille 1d
glass verre 10b
glasses lunettes 19d
glove gant 19a
go aller 3a; allez 1c
good bon 6a; beau 17b
good afternoon bonjour 1b
goodbye au revoir 1b
good morning bonjour 1b
go on passer 2a
grape raisin 13b
gravel gravillons 4
gravy sauce 12b
grey gris 19c
green vert 19c
grocer's épicerie 9
ground floor rez-de-chaussée 6b

guarded surveillé 3d
guest house pension de famille 6a
guide guide 15d

hail grêle 17c
haircut coupe 19e
hairdresser coiffeur 19e
half demi 8a
half an hour demi-heure 8a
half-bottle demi-bouteille 14b
ham jambon 10d
hand main 20e
handbag sac 2a
handkerchief mouchoir 19d
hat chapeau 19a
headache mal à la tête 20e
heart attack crise cardiaque 20d
heavy vehicles poids lourds 3a
hello bonjour 1b; allô 18c; salut 1b
help secours 20g
high-pressure area anticyclone 17b
hire louer 16c
hospital hôpital 20d
hot chaud 17b
hotel hôtel 6a
hour heure 8a
house maison 4b
how comment 1b
how many combien 7b/11a
how much combien 3c/6c/9d
hurt blessé 20e
husband mari 1f

I je 1f
ice verglas 17d
ice cream glace 13d
iced glacé 13b
ill malade 20e
indigestion indigestion 20e
information information 5e
injured blessé 20e
insurance assurance 20a
island île 16b

jacket veste 19a
jam confiture 10c
jug carafe 10b
juice jus 10c/14a
July juillet 8c

English-French Vocabulary

key clé 1f/6b/20b
knife couteau 10b

ladies dames 6d
lake lac 16b
lamb agneau 12b
lawyer avocat 20c
left gauche 4d
left luggage consigne 5a
leg of lamb gigot 12b
lemon citron 10c/13b/14a
letter lettre 18b
letter box boîte aux lettres 18a
lettuce salade 13a
lift ascenseur 6b
lighter briquet 14c
liqueur liqueur 14b
liver pâté pâté de foie 12b
local trains trains de banlieue 5a
lockers consigne automatique 5a
long long 19a
long-distance trains grandes lignes 5a
lorry camion 3a
lose perdre 20b
low-pressure area dépression 17c
luggage bagages 2a
lunch déjeuner 10a

mackerel maquereau 12d
madam madame 1a
main lines grandes lignes 5a
man homme 1d
map carte 4a
market marché 9c
marmalade confiture 10c
match allumette 14c
meal repas 10a
meat viande 12b
medicine médicament 20f
Mediterranean Méditerranée 16b
medium à point 12b
melon melon 13b
men messieurs 6d
menu carte 11b
midnight minuit 8b
milk lait 7b/10c/14a
miss mademoiselle 1d/11d

Monday lundi 8c
money argent 9a
month mois 8c
morning matin 8a/8b
motorway autoroute 3b
motel motel 6a
mountain montagne 16b
mountain-climbing alpinisme 16c
Mr monsieur 1d
Mrs madame 1d
museum musée 15b
mushroom champignon 13a
mussels moules 12d
my ma, mon 1f

name nom 1f/2b
napkin serviette 10b
nationality nationalité 2c
near tout près 4d
newspaper journal 2c
night nuit 6b/8b
night club boîte de nuit 15c
no non 1a/2a
noon midi 8b
north nord 4d
now maintenant

obligatory obligatoire 3d
offence contravention 20c
oil huile 3c/11c
ointment pommade 20f
one-way street sens unique 4c
onion oignon 12a/13a
open ouvert 15d
opening hours heures d'ouverture 15d
or ou 14c
orange orange 13b
orange juice orangeade 14a
order commander 11b
outing excursion 16a
overcast couvert 17c
oysters huîtres 12d

packet of cigarettes paquet de cigarettes 14c
pair of shoes paire de chaussures 19b

English-French Vocabulary

palace château 15b/16a; palais 15b
pancake crêpe 10d/12c
park jardin 16b
parking stationnement 3d
parking disc disque 3d
parking lot parking 3d
passport passeport 2b
pastry pâtisserie 13c
pay payer 6c/9d
pear poire 13b
peas pois 13a
pedal boat pédalo 16c
pepper poivre 11c
performance spectacle 15c
petrol essence 3c
pharmacy pharmacie 20f
photo photo 16d
pilgrimage pélerinage 15b
place of residence domicile 2b
plaster sparadrap 20f
plate assiette 10b
platform voie 5a
please s'il vous plaît 1c
police police; gendarmerie 20c
policeman agent de police 20c
pork porc 12b
port port 5c
postcard carte postale 18b
post code code postale 18b
post office bureau de poste 18a
potatoes pommes de terre 13a
pound livre 9b
price prix 6c/9d
pull tirez 15d
pullman couchettes 5a
purse porte-monnaie 20b
push poussez 15d

quarter of an hour quart d'heure 8a
quick vite 20f

raincoat imperméable 19a
railways chemins de fer 5a
rain pluie 17c
raspberries framboises 13b
rapid transit R.E.R. 5d
rare saignant 12b
receiver récepteur 18c

reception desk réception 6b
red rouge 19c
regular ordinaire 3c
report signaler 20a
reserve réserver 6b
reservation réservation 5a
rib steak entrecôte 12b
rice riz 13a
right droite 4d
right-of-way priorité 3b
river rivière 16b
road route 3b
road toll péage 3b
road works travaux 3b
roast rôti 12c
rock rocher 16b
room chambre 6b
room number numéro de chambre 6b
runner beans haricots verts 13a

sail board planche à voile 16c
sailing boat voilier 16c
saling school école de voile 16c
salt sel 11c
sanitary towel serviette hygiénique 19d
Saturday samedi 18c
sausage saucisse 10d
scarf foulard 19a
Scotland Ecosse 2c
Scottish Ecossais/e 2c
sea mer 16b
see visiter 15b/15d
self-service libre-service 9c
sender expéditeur 18b
serious grave 20f
service service 11d
service station station-service 3c
set meal menu 11b
shade ombre 17b
shampoo shampooing 19d
shellfish fruits de mer 12d
ship bateau 5c
shirt chemise 9a/19a
shoes chaussures 19b
shop magasin 9c
short court 19a

English-French Vocabulary

shower douche 6b; averse 17c
shrimps crevettes 12d
sights curiosités 15b
sightseeing tour tour de ville 4b
size taille 19a; pointure 19b
skirt jupe 19a
sky ciel 17c
sleeping car wagon-lit 5a
sleeping pill somnifère 20f
slow down ralentir 3b
small change monnaie 9a
smart chic 19a
smoke fumer 14c
snails escargots 12b
snow neige 17d
soap savon 19d
socks chaussettes 19b
sole sole 12d
soup soupe, potage 12a
soup bowl soupière 10b
south sud 4d
spoon cuiller 10b
square place 4c
stadium stade 15c
stairs escalier 6b
stamp timbre 18b
station gare 5a
steal voler 20b
stew ragoût 12b
stockings bas 19b
storey étage 6b
stop attendez 4c
straight ahead tout droit 4d
strawberry fraise 10c/13b
street rue 4c/4d
street map plan 4a
stroll promenade 16c
sugar sucre 11c/13b
suitcase valise 1e/1f
sun soleil 17b
sunburn coup de soleil 20e
Sunday dimanche 8c
suntan oil huile solaire 19d
supermarket supermarché 9c
supper dîner 10a; souper 10a
sweater pull-over 19a
sweet bonbon 13c
swim nager 16c

swimming costume maillot de bain 19a
swimming pool piscine 16c
Switzerland Suisse 2c

table table 11a
tablecloth nappe 10b
tablet comprimé 20f
take prendre 19a
tan bronzer 16c
tart tarte 13c
taxi taxi 5d
tea thé 10c/14a; goûter 10a
tea shop salon de thé 11a
teeth dents 20e
telephone book annuaire 18c
telephone box cabine téléphonique 18c
telephone number numéro de téléphone 18c
thank you merci 1c/9c
the le, la, les 1e
theatre théâtre 15c
thief voleur 20b
this ce, cette 1e
thunderstorm orage 17c
Thursday jeudi 8c
ticket billet 5a/15d
ticket office guichet 5a
ticket window caisse 15d
tight étroit 19a
tights collant 19b
timetable horaire 5e
tip pourboire 11d
tissues mouchoirs de papier 19d
to jusqu à 7b
toasted sandwich croque-monsieur 10d
tobacconist bureau de tabac 14c
today aujourd'hut 8b
toilets toilettes 6d
tomorrow demain 8b
toothbrush brosse à dents 19d
toothpaste dentifrice 19d
tour visiter 15b/15d; circuit 16a
tourist information office syndicat d'initiative 15a
towel serviette de toilette 19d

English-French Vocabulary

tower tour 15b
town ville 4b
town hall hôtel de ville 4b
track voie 5a
traffic circulation 3a
traffic light feu rouge 4c
train train 5a
travel agency agence de voyages
    15a
traveller's cheque chèque de voyage
    9b
trip voyage 1e
trousers pantalon 19a
truck camion 3a
Tuesday mardi 8c
turn tournez 4d
tyres pneus 3c

umbrella parapluie 17c
underground métro 5d
underground station station de
    métro 5d
understand comprendre 2c

vacant libre 6d
vantage point point de vue 16a
veal veau 12b
veal cutlet escalope 12b
vegetables légumes 13a
very much beaucoup 1c
village village 4b
visit visiter 15b/15d

waiter garçon 11d
waiting room salle d'attente 5a

Wales pays de Galles 2c
walk promenade 16c
wallet portefeuille 20b
warm chaud 17b
watch montre 8a
water eau 10b/17b
water skiing ski nautique 16c
weather temps 17a
weather forecast météo 17a
Wednesday mercredi 8c
week semaine 8c
well bien 1b/2a
well-done bien cuit 12b
Welsh Gallois/e 2c
west ouest 4d
when quand 8b
where où 4c/4d/5d/6a/15a/18a
white blanc 19c
wife femme 1f
wind vent 17c
wine vin 10b/14b
wine list carte des vins 11b
with avec 6b/14c
without sans 14c
woman femme 1d
wood bois 16b

yellow jaune 19c
yes oui 1a/2a
yesterday hier 8b
you vous 1f
your votre 1f
youth hostel auberge de la jeunesse
    6a

Teach Yourself edition first published 1986
Second impression 1986
Copyright © 1986
Hodder and Stoughton Ltd

Translated and adapted from the original German edition by
Shirley Baldwin. German edition by Diethard Lübke, copyright ©
1983 by Langenscheidt KG, Berlin and Munich.
Illustrations by Herbert Horn.

British Library Cataloguing in Publication Data

Lubke, Diethard
 Quick and easy French.—(Teach yourself books)
 1. French language—Spoken French
 I. Title
 448.3′421   PC2121

 ISBN 0 340 38764 5

Printed and bound in Great Britain for
Hodder and Stoughton Educational,
a division of Hodder and Stoughton Ltd,
Mill Road, Dunton Green, Sevenoaks, Kent,
by Fletcher & Son Ltd, Norwich

Phototypeset by Macmillan India Ltd, Bangalore 25